I HOPE MY MOTHER DOESN'T READ THIS

A Collection of Humorous Essays

GREG SCARNICI

Dear Jeff & Meryl,

I hope you still talk to me
after reading this.

love,

Thought Catalog Books
Brooklyn, NY

THOUGHT CATALOG BOOKS

Copyright © 2015 by Greg Scarnici

All rights reserved. Published by Thought Catalog Books, a division of
The Thought & Expression Co., Williamsburg, Brooklyn.

For general information and submissions: hello@thoughtcatalog.com.

First edition, 2015.
ISBN 978-0692521472
10 9 8 7 6 5 4 3 2 1

Founded in 2010, Thought Catalog is a website and imprint dedicated
to your ideas and stories. We publish fiction and non-fiction from
emerging and established writers across all genres.

Cover photography by © Daniella Urdinlaiz

Dedicated to Paul Regan, who, for some reason,

put up with me during most of this.

CONTENTS

DISCLAIMER

Some of the names have been changed to protect the
guilty.

FOREWARD

I started writing this collection in 2008, and a lot of it covers the late 80s and early 90s, a time when I was just starting to understand my sexuality and discover this city of New York I call my home. Looking back, in many ways, the two were intertwined. Growing up in Queens, New York gave me access to the streets and nightclubs of NYC, which I was drawn to ever since my cousin, Frankie, told me about evenings at Studio 54 when I was six years old. I idolized him as a child, as he had no shame in being openly gay at a time when it wasn't so acceptable.

Nowadays, boys practically cartwheel out of their mother's vaginas and scream, "I'm gay!" and the video of their performance lands them 1.5 million likes on Facebook and an appearance on *Ellen*. But back then, we didn't have every celebrity championing for our rights on social media, or any media for that matter.

But thankfully, a lot of that has changed. The acceptance of LGBT people across the nation is now within our grasp, and children are not riddled with as much self-hate when they discover they just might be different from their classmates as people of my generation were. In fact, today, all an infant needs to do is reach for a Barbie doll, and his parents will start running around the house, screaming, "John's transgender! We're putting him on estrogen when he's five!"

The rest of this book covers another period of struggle in my life, when I did not yet achieve the level of success I have recently started to, thanks to YouTube and people who find a kindred spirit in my left of center brand of comedy. Back then, I clamored for acceptance in the world of mainstream comedy, which was largely controlled by straight men who did not share my sensibilities. As you will discover, trying to change my creative expression did not get me anywhere. It took me years to realize my best work came from expressing my unique identity, and not trying to write for Will Ferrell.

Thanks to the Internet, there is now a place for artists of all types to create work and find an audience. And since LGBT people are currently going through a civil rights movement, gay, bi and trans artists are a lot more accepted in society. In fact, check your local listings – there's probably a "Transsexual Bachelor/ette" on ABC tonight!

As I look back on all those years of thinking I was completely and utterly talentless, I realize I needed that time to learn to love my creative self without the need for outside validation, just like I needed to learn to love myself without caring about what anyone thought years ago. But then again, outside validation *is* nice, so rate this book five stars or I might just go down another shame spiral. Thanks. You're the best!

- Greg Scarnici, May, 2015

CHAPTER 1.

EXTRA, EXTRA!

"You look nervous."
  "I look nervous?"
  "Yes, you look nervous."
  "Yes, I look nervous?"
  "Yes, you look nervous."
  "You look nervous."
  "I look nervous?"
  "Yes, you look nervous."
  "Fine, I look nervous."
  "Fine, you look nervous?"
  "Yes, fine, I look nervous."
  "*Yes*, fine, you look nervous."
  "Fuck you."
  "Fuck you, too."

The preceding dialogue would be applauded as wonderful, truthful and honest in any Meisner-based acting studio in New York City. Repetition, as *any* well-trained actor knows, is an exercise created by Sanford Meisner, also known to a select group of assholes as "Sandy." The premise of the exercise is to make actors listen to their partner so they can hear what they are trying to convey and react to it. The idea seems infantile to me, as I am always aware of how people react to me in everyday life. When I'm telling someone a story and they start scrolling through Instagram, I can pretty much tell I've lost them. I'm very much in tune with how people respond to me, and like the insecure mess I am, alter my behavior accordingly. Not so for your typical actor. For people who are supposed to be able to read body language and pick up on signals, most of them are blind.

For this reason, repetition always annoyed me, while the rest of my classmates found it "earth shattering," "amazing," and, "the key to their craft." This is because most actors do not listen when other people speak. To them, conversation is perceived as interactive theater in which *they are the stars!*

This first became apparent when I started taking acting classes at The William Esper Studio on West 37th Street. A few times a month, I would be forced to meet up with actresses outside of class to rehearse scenes. I quickly learned that "I just need a cup of coffee" roughly translated to: "I will now talk about how my boyfriend is distant during sex" for an hour and a half. These therapy sessions always ended with them asking me what they should do, and their eyes glazing over as I offered advice they would never take because they weren't even listening. Instead, they were rehearsing the next monologue they planned on unleashing upon me. After an hour of "conversing," the time would come for them to rush off to their restaurant shift and we'd never get to rehearse.

When the time came to do our scenes in class, they always threw the concept of listening out the window and simply performed the scene as they imagined it should be while ignoring the customers who were trying to get their checks at the restaurant the night before. "I'll look him in the eye and then turn away when I say that line! Then I'll leave in a huff, turn my head quickly, and say that last line!" It was as if all of their acting instincts came from watching Krystal Carrington fight Alexis Morrell-Carrington-Colby-Dexter-Rowan on reruns of *Dynasty*.

At the end of our scene, my partner would exit with a dramatic flourish to the applause of the other students and our acting teacher, who commended their performance for being "in the moment." I can safely say most of these acting teachers don't even watch these scenes because they're too busy fantasizing about that "recurring role" they once had on *Days of Our Lives* as a nurse. At the end of class, my partner would embrace me, and say, "I lost myself in that scene! It was magical!" Then she'd rush off to therapy.

Besides therapy appointments, a lot of my acting partners also had acupuncture sessions we had to work around. They each sought the help of acupuncturists, herbalists, and holistic doctors for pains in their stomach, arms, legs, and various other body parts. They told me these pains came from years of serving food, but I always believed they were physical manifestations of mental anguish. So stop wearing that magnetic copper bracelet around your left wrist to help with the sciatica that shoots "lightning bolts of pain" down your right thigh and STFU.

Another hypocritical thing about actors is that even though their art supposedly trains them to live openly and freely, most of them are paranoid. They watch their every move and second-guess every decision. While having lunch at The Waverly Restaurant with one of my scene partners, she'd say, "Hmmm, maybe I should have ordered the turkey club – no, turkey makes me sooooooooo tired – I'm glad I got the tuna melt – although that mercury is going to be the death of me…I told you my mother has cervical cancer, right? I'm gonna change my order. Waiter!! Waiter!!…Why is he ignoring me? Was I rude to him? Did you see me be rude to him?" "He's not ignoring you – he's taking someone else's order." "Oh, thank God, I thought I was rude to him – I would hate that, because I'm a waiter, and I know what it's like to be abused by a customer. During brunch the other day, this woman had the *nerve*…" "Aaaaaaahhhhh!" I'd scream in my head – "Can we just rehearse the scene so I can get the fuck out of here?"

All of the nuances, ticks, and mannerisms of these actors were perfectly captured in a Columbia student film I once acted in, called "Extras." The opening shot of the film panned across forty actors who were waiting to audition for extra work in a feature film. To add absurdity to the scene, the casting call had everyone show up in black tie and formal gowns. The camera tracked across their faces as they said one or two lines that summed up what losers they were…in tuxedos and sequined pant suits. The ironic thing was that everyone who got cast in this film loved to talk about how pathetic their character was and how they would never be caught dead doing extra work. These people were so blind, they couldn't see the film they were acting in (for free) was lampooning their very existence. They weren't even working on a *feature film!!!* that would help them get points towards earning their SAG card, or whatever the fuck actors convince themselves doing extra work on real films will get them.

As far as I was concerned, no role was beneath me. Actor friends would say, "I can't do extra work. It's just so demoralizing." What they really meant was, "I can't do extra work. I'm not the center of attention." I had no problem showing up to be a stockbroker, or a customer in a café, even though I knew it would be a 12-hour day. Sure, there would be a lot of down time and it wouldn't be that stimulating, but I'd be on a movie set or in a TV studio! And with all that time on my hands, I'd be able to sequence all those on-the-go playlists and text friends who were working in cubicles! "Margaret Cho got fat," I texted Jessica, who was making phone calls trying to enlist people to donate money for whatever non-profit she was working for that month. "Ben Stiller's an asshole," I texted Kevin, who was…doing whatever people who work in finance do.

That's why the irony of playing a pathetic actor trying to get extra work in a student film was not lost on me. I found the whole experience surreal. Especially when some of the actors ran around talking about how their "agent" landed them this part, which consisted of showing up at a warehouse in Harlem at 8AM on a rainy Saturday morning for free.

As fate would have it, I wound up being teamed with an actress who was undoubtedly the dramatic world's biggest disaster. Agatha Bromley – who apparently never heard of the concept of stage names – played a jaded actress who frowns upon my character's naiveté when I ask her if she's nervous. It was an interchange of two lines, but you would have thought we were delivering Shakespearean monologues by the way she tortured herself over the delivery of this *one line*. "Should I be more condescending? No, I think it's fine the way it is. Wait, can we try it again? I think I'm going to try it *cavalier.*" We'd run our lines and she'd analyze how "the scene" went as the crew worked out technical kinks between rehearsals.

To add realness to the scene, the director had us hold our actual headshots while we waited to meet with the casting director. Within a minute, Agatha leaned over to analyze mine. "Wow, yours is a 3/4 body shot. Mine's just a face. I should totally re-do mine. Hmm. Is that font Helvetica? I used Times. Do you think it's too old fashioned? Should I re-do it?" she asked. "Calm down!" I wanted to shout. "It's 8:30 in the fucking morning!"

Agatha lived in the West Village with her boyfriend and her cat, which was so fucked up from living with her that the poor thing was on Prozac. Every morning, she and her boyfriend took turns cutting the pills in half and shoving them into the cat's bowl of Fancy Feast. They even kept a calendar marking whose day it was to medicate it. Why one person couldn't be in charge of this was beyond me. Why complicate matters? But complicating things was Agatha's specialty. "The camera tracks us from stage left. We should clock our bodies so our faces get more screen time." Stage left? We were in a hallway in an abandoned warehouse. Screen time? This was a student film that *might* be seen by the director's teacher if he was able to round up the money to edit it, which would probably not be the case, judging from the looks of the craft service table.

As we stood in line rehearsing this shot over and over again, she told me about her acting classes at the T. Schreiber Studio, how her manager stopped representing her *for some reason*, how her boyfriend broke up with her but she convinced him to come back, and how she missed her mother in Michigan. In order to entertain myself, I started adding lines to my "scene" each time we rehearsed. My original line read, "I just moved to the city and this is my first audition. Are you nervous?" After the first run-through, it now read, "Jeepers! I just moved to the city and now I'm acting full time. This is my first audition. Isn't that great?" As the director passed us after each rehearsal, he'd smirk and then turn to Agatha, who awaited his approval as if her very life depended on it.

"Why don't you try it a little warmer," he told her at first, which I knew was code for, "you are stiff and lifeless." Then she'd turn to me, make me rehearse the "scene" again and "change" the way she did it. After mind numbing passes at our "scene," I was convinced this woman had no versatility. I, on the other hand, had morphed my line to read, "Can you believe I just moved to New York City and now I'm an actor? I am so stoked. I've been taking classes at HB Studios and I'm just *thrilled to pieces* to be here auditioning for a *feature film!* Dreams really do come true, don't you think?" As the director passed by for his final list of notes, he told me, "That's enough," and turned to Agatha — who was still stiff as a clapboard – and said, "Uh, fine," which I knew was code for "I give up."

Since the scene was technical, I was forced to stand next to this energy vacuum for three more hours until they were able to get it right. When we were done, I dragged my carcass back to the abandoned office that served as the staging area to change.

Ten minutes later, I was on the platform of the 1 train waiting to go home. I looked down the station to see if the train was coming, only to spot a train wreck headed my way. I ducked behind a column, hoping to avoid her, but it was too late.

"He told me I had potential," she said dejectedly.

"Huh?" I asked.

"The director. I asked him what he thought of my performance and he told me I had potential. What's that supposed to mean? Was I *that* bad?" she asked.

"I don't think so," I lied. Why in the world was this 35-year-old woman seeking the approval of a student director? I personally knew most of them were so overburdened with the prospect of shooting a film, they don't even watch their actors. They're too busy worrying about losing their next location or where the money's going to come from for that late night pizza run.

As we stepped into the subway for a painful 30-minute ride downtown, I told myself I would never do extra work again. And not because I was afraid of *not* being the center of attention, but because I just might *become* someone's center of attention.

CHAPTER 2.

BOOBY HATCHED

Recently, I saw Liza Minnelli in the concert film, *Liza With A Z*. Although I was amazed by her exuberant performance, I found myself more transfixed by the insane look that came across her face every fifteen minutes or so. While hoofing her way through "Ring Them Bells," or singing "God Bless The Child," a random emotion would possess her and the look of a crazed maniac would flash across the screen. At one point, I was certain a drag queen had escaped from an asylum and had taken her place on stage.

Towards the end of the movie, as Liza sang a bizarre version of "Mammy," a rabid look in her eyes conjured an image of my bipolar cousin running around her apartment after one of her $3,000 shopping binges. At that moment, I realized there's a thin line between being a genius and mentally ill. In fact, in many performers, the traits are undoubtedly intertwined. So the next time you catch Liza trumping out "New York, New York" on *The View*, ask yourself – is she talented, crazy, or both?

CHAPTER 3.

ENCORE!

Whenever I shoot a film, there's always one person in the cast or crew I bond with. A kindred spirit, if you will. Since most actors are complete neurotics and most of the gaffers are fresh out of jail, there's always a plethora of interesting people to choose from. On a short film I once acted in called "Stakeout," that person wound up being an incredibly attractive actor named Derek. An ex-model who looked like Tommy Lee, I would lose myself in his eyes as we rehearsed. After the film wrapped, we talked on the phone, telling each other about auditions we thought the other might be right for. Then we'd talk about ourselves as only self-absorbed actors can. Each phone call always ended the same – with Derek saying, "Dude, we have *got* to hang out."

Three months later, we finally did. One cold October night, my boyfriend, Paul and I were at a karaoke bar with our friends when I saw Derek pop up on my caller ID. He was at home, having cocktails with his roommate, trying to figure out what to do with the rest of the night. When I told him we were at a karaoke bar, he told me he'd be there in an hour.

What passed through the door two hours later can only be described as the spawn of Courtney Love and The Crypt Keeper. Derek and his roommate, Michael, a short, pudgy fellow with a stuttering problem and a lisp, had obviously been "having cocktails" for the past two days. I figured they were also doing cocaine, since there were remnants of a rock in his goatee.

I introduced the two of them to my horrified friends, who had sworn off drugs years ago and were simply content being alcoholics. After looking over a book of songs trying to help Derek pick one out, my friend Jessica pulled me aside and asked, "Where did you dig up Corpse Breath?" I quickly reminded her that people on coke binges generally do not eat or brush their teeth since it's hard to remember to do those things when you don't sleep. As an ex-Ritalin lover, she understood completely and offered him a stick of Wrigley's.

Derek insisted on singing a duet with her, who was repulsed to learn they would have to share a microphone. Derek was a huge Disney fan and decided to sing "Somewhere Out There." As soon as the song started, Jessica was thrilled to learn he went into a zone somewhere in the stratosphere when he "sang" and lost all semblance of reality. She quickly slithered away and let him take center stage.

As the opening chords played, he closed his eyes, gripped the microphone and started to sing/whisper the song in a kind of Janet Jackson falsetto. The intensity of his performance was captivating. He definitely related with the plight of poor Fievel Mousekewitz and was able to emote the song beautifully. He wasn't a great singer, but you couldn't take your eyes off him. He was like the karoake equivalent of one of those videos that pop on Facebook of white people dancing at music festivals.

While he was singing, his roommate seized the opportunity to pull me aside and inquire about our "relationship."

"So how-how-how-how long have you known Derek?" he stuttered.

"Uh, I don't know, a few months." I said.

"He talks about you all the time you kn-kn-kn-know," he said.

"Oh, really," I said.

"He thaid you're an a-a-a-a-a-amazing actor."

"Well he's something else, too," I said as Derek reached a note I thought humanly impossible.

"I know he is. He's incredible. He's going to be a star. A big, big star," he said as he watched him longingly. At that moment, I realized Michael was in love with Derek. "I've lived with him for eight years and he's the best actor in the world. I've seen everything he's ever done. The play when he played the ex-con, that other play when he played that other ex-con, and that musical when he played a drug addict." Apparently, Derek had quite the range.

Michael seemed to lose his stutter when he spoke of his enamored. "You're not interested in him, are you?" he asked.

"I'm here with my boyfriend," I told him. A giant smile spread across his face. "Oh...Derek never mentioned him," he said. By this time, the song ended and I excused myself to sing "Raspberry Beret." When I finished, I found out Derek and his roommate had left. He called the next day to say his roommate got a sudden case of diarrhea. And by "sudden case of diarrhea," he really meant, "went to buy more drugs." He asked me if I wanted to meet him at a karaoke bar later that week. It was in the heart of Times Square, and chorus boys often frequented the bar to grab the spotlight from leads after Broadway shows. "Dude, we gotta hit that fuckin' place. You'll fuckin' kill there," he said.

"I'm kind of karaoke-d out, so maybe in a few weeks?" I said.

Around Christmas, he phoned again. "Dude, you've gotta get your ass over here. We're going to karaoke and it's gonna be a blast. Come to our place first and we'll have holiday cocktails," he said. Against my better judgment I decided, "What the hell?" I hopped on the D train and arrived at his apartment on W48th Street around 9 o'clock. I rang the doorbell. Once. Twice. Three times. No answer. I tried calling him on his cell. No answer. I tried the bell one more time, and finally got buzzed inside.

When I reached his fifth floor walk-up, I was "greeted" by his roommate, Michael. He let me into the apartment and just stared at me. "Hey, how are you? It's good to see you again," I said.

"D-D-Derek will be out in a mi-mi-mi-mi-mi-nu-nu-te," he stuttered as he stormed into his bedroom and slammed the door. Something was wrong. I sat down and stared at a Charlie Brown Christmas tree which had dried out weeks ago. Frank Sinatra's depressing Christmas CD was playing as I looked around their dreary living room. This was turning out to be one festive holiday get-together.

Five minutes later, Derek opened the door to his bedroom, which was basically the dining room of their railroad apartment. The first thing I noticed was that his pants were unzipped. Behind him stood a man with a dopey smirk on his face. "Hey, Gee, what's going on?" he asked as he tried to kiss me on the lips. I turned my cheek just in time and realized he had penis breath. "Yeah, cool, chill out, I'll make us a few drinks," he said.

"Who's your friend?" I asked.

"Oh, this is…what the fuck is your name again, dude?" Derek slurred.

"Mike," the stranger replied.

"Right, Mike. Mike's on break. He works at Burger King," Derek said without any sense of irony.

"Yeah, gotta go. I'm gonna be late," Mike said as he bolted out the door.

"Meet up with us later. We're gonna be at Cleo's!" Derek screamed down the hallway.

"Gee, man, it's so good to see you. You're lookin' great." He stepped in closer for a kiss. I sidestepped him and sat on the couch. "Who the hell was that?" I asked. "Oh, some dude I met online. I was in the mood to give head. Still am." He smiled and reached over to run his hand up my leg. As if on cue, his roommate burst through the door and lunged at us.

"I th-th-th-th-th-th-thought you had a b-b-b-b-b-oyfriend," he snapped.

"I do," I told him.

"Then Derek, you thould get your hand off him," he lisped.

"Dude, you are so right. I am so sorry. I'll go make us drinks. Vodka and cranberry good?" he asked as he walked into the kitchen. Michael stood, just staring at me. "Hey, chop up that rock and let's party!" Derek screamed from the kitchen. Michael got down on his knees and started cutting up the coke that was lying on a vanity mirror on the coffee table.

"I can't be-be-be-be-believe him. That's the th-th-th-third person he's had over here to-to-to-to-night," he informed me. "And to-to-to-to-night was supposed to be th-th-th-th-special. I pr-pr-pr-pr-pr-pr-proposed to him before you got here," he added. Did he just stutter what I thought he stuttered? And when did this take place? Between blowjobs?

"Oh, really?" I asked.

"He kn-kn-kn-knows I love him. He just doesn't kn-kn-kn-know that he loves me y-y-y-y-yet," he said. It was true. I was in the gay *Fatal Attraction*.

"Hey, Gee, get the fuck in here and help me with these drinks," Derek screamed from the kitchen. Grateful to be relieved of the bizarre Lifetime movie unfolding in the living room, I headed to the kitchen. Derek was in the middle of making drinks with a plastic bottle of Georgi and White Label Iced Tea Powder. "What's going on with Michael?" I asked him.

"What'd he tell you – about that whole marriage thing? He's whacked out of his mind," he said. "So what's up? You gonna let me suck that hot Italian cock of yours or what?" he asked. It was true. Derek was Shakespeare reincarnated.

I looked over and saw Michael peering into the doorway from the couch in the living room. "I'll be back," Derek said. He walked over to the kitchen and slammed the door, leaving Michael by himself in the living room. He stumbled back over and placed his hand on my crotch. "So what's up man? You gonna let me hit this or what?" he asked. I could not believe he was actually coming onto me after blowing Mike from Burger King and whoever was behind Doors #1 and #2. "Derek, you know I have a boyfriend. And besides, you have a wedding proposal to consider."

Bang bang! "What the f-f-f-f-f-fuck's going on in there?" Michael screamed from the living room.

"Dude, take it easy. You want a drink?" Derek yelled back. "Yeah, and h-h-h-h-h-hurry up," he snap/stuttered.

"One second dude, I just gotta mix up some more ice tea," Derek screamed back.

"H-h-h-h-urry up, I've cued up your acting reel."

"Cool!" Derek said. A few minutes later, we headed into the living room to watch Derek's acting reel. As I looked out of the corner of my eye, I caught a glimpse of Michael mouthing the words to one of the scenes. This guy had nothing on Glenn Close.

Derek sat down next to me and started rubbing my leg again. Had he no shame or short-term memory? Michael glanced over and screamed, "We n-n-n-n-n-need to talk. Now! In the k-k-k-k-k-k-k-k-k-k-k-kk-k-k-k-kitchen, Derek."

"Dude, I'll be back in a minute. Help yourself to some blow," Derek said as he rolled his eyes and headed off. A few seconds later, they were in the middle of a screaming match which rivaled anything seen on *Cops*. Michael berated Derek for a host of horrible things he did to him *just that day* and Derek tried to appease him. It was painfully obvious Derek took advantage of Michael's love.

I used this opportunity to phone my friend, John, who was waiting to meet us at a piano bar down the street. "I'm sorry I'm late, but I'll explain when I see you," I told him. "No problem, although you are missing a captivating number from 'Annie Get Your Gun'" he replied. "See you in a few," I told him as I hung up.

Two minutes later, Derek and Michael emerged from the kitchen. "What's up, Gee? You need another drink?" Derek said, as if nothing had happened.

"No, I'm actually gonna get out of here. My friend is waiting for me at Judy's Turn. You wanna come?"

"Nah, it would be weird to meet your friends like this," he replied. Apparently, he had no recollection of meeting them a few months ago. I guess he really was "Somewhere Out There."

"But I'll see you at karaoke later on, right?" he added.

"Yeah, I'll call you in a little while." I got the hell out of there and met up with John, who was intrigued about what was going on back at Derek's apartment. "I have got to meet this guy," he said. "He sounds fascinating. We're going to that karaoke bar," he demanded.

We made our way over to Cleo's an hour later. As we got to the front of the bar, my cell phone rang. It was Derek. "Yo, Gee, come up to the apartment. We took the party back to my place," he said. Afraid of stepping back into another scene from *Who's Afraid of Virginia Woolf*, I declined. John grabbed the cell phone out of my hand and told Derek we'd be there in a minute. "Cool, man, just pick up some Georgi. There's a liquor store on 46th and 8th," he told this person he never met.

When we finally crawled back into their dungeon of an apartment with a bottle of Smirnoff (John had standards), Derek was in the midst of entertaining yet *another* guy he met at Cleo's. Michael was seething in the corner as Derek danced around the living room. The soundtrack to *Chicago* was playing, and Derek was now wearing just a pair of tighty whities and an undershirt. The new guy introduced himself as Sean, and told us Derek lured him back to the apartment with the promise of a blowjob.

Instead, he put on the soundtrack to *Chicago* and started performing each song, complete with choreography, as he slowly peeled off his clothes. Michael chimed in that we had just missed a captivating performance of "I Can't Do It Alone." I guess Derek was able to do it alone.

Just then, "Razzle Dazzle" came on and Derek jumped up, ready to perform. Michael beamed and told us this was one of his favorite numbers in Derek's "repertoire." He started dancing in his underwear while pulling up his guinea T to "razzle dazzle" us at just the right moments. He was singing in that bizarre falsetto again, and was clearly "in the moment." What else would explain him knocking over the Christmas tree and not noticing?

I looked at John, who realized we had stepped into a horror film. He later told me he felt like we were transported into that scene in *Boogie Nights* when Markie Mark and his friends go to that crack head's house who sings "Sister Christian" while firecrackers go off.

Michael sidled up to John to cry on his shoulder about his proposal being refused. John tried to be sympathetic, even though Derek was straddling his new friend not five feet away. *Somehow,* Derek lost his balance and crashed to the floor. Something needed to be done. I pulled him to his feet and carried him to his room. As I placed him on the bed, he roused from his inebriated state and came onto me again.

"Hey, Gee, take off those pants and let me go to town on that dick," he slurred. He was like a monster in a horror movie who refused to die. "Just go to sleep," I told him. When I got back to the living room, John already had his coat on. "Well, Greg, it's about that time. I do have a matinee tomorrow, you know," which was code for, "Let's get the fuck out of here." I got my coat and said goodnight to Sean, who seemed oblivious to everything going on around him. As we headed for the door, Derek rose from the dead and emerged from his room.

"Where you guys goin'? We're just getting started!" he announced. Apparently this show had a few more acts. Just then, "Class" came on and Derek started dancing over to us in just his underwear. The irony was not lost on either of us. A performer through and through, Derek was not going to miss his encore. "Quick. Bolt," John said as I slammed the door in Derek's face.

When we reached the street, John threw his scarf around his neck and asked me, "Where did you meet that guy again?" I summed it all up when I told him, "On that film I found on Craigslist."

CHAPTER 4.

LIVE FROM NEW YORK

As soon as I graduated with a Film Degree from Hunter College, I mapped out my plan to break into the entertainment industry. It was my design to get a job as a PA on a TV show, work my way up until I was writing, and then segue into writing and directing films by the time I was thirty. A good plan... that didn't work. Although I did get a job working in TV, that whole "working my way up the ladder" thing never happened. Breaks never came my way, but that didn't stop me – I just kept plodding along like a bumbling idiot. Although the idea I was totally talentless crossed my mind many, many times, I could not stop writing, directing, acting and making music because being creative was just a part of who I was. Come hell or high water, I would be doing this for the rest of my life.

The first stop in my plan was getting a job at *Saturday Night Live*. That long-running variety show was the perfect place to be for a host of reasons. First off, it was a comedy show, which is what I loved doing for as long as I could remember. Ever since I was a child, my sister Diane and I put on lounge acts for our family every Christmas

Eve. I would play the corny host as she sang, "Go Tell It On The Mountain" as a three hundred pound woman with pillows under her skirt. Or I would prance around in a black cat suit as she sang "Vogue." To think my family was not aware of my sexual orientation at the time boggles me to this day.

When I was seven, the two of us invented a British brother/sister act who scored a Top Ten Hit with our song, "Cuckoo Clock." We'd run around family parties, forcing cousins to interview us as we went "'roun' the states" promoting our single. During the interview, we'd cut them off as we burst into another rendition of "Cuckoo Clock," annoying everyone around.

Years later, it came as no surprise when I took a playwriting course at Hunter College and one of my classmates critiqued a scene of mine by saying it sounded like a sketch on *Saturday Night Live*. She thought she was insulting me, but I was thrilled! The cornerstone of her craft might have stemmed from Shakespeare, but mine came from The Sweenie Sisters.

The other reason I was drawn to *Saturday Night Live* was because it was based in New York. Although I loved the entertainment industry, I had no interest in moving to Los Angeles. Sure the weather was great, but as a New Yorker, I had a hard time clicking with people whenever I visited. I knew this was because most of the people I encountered probably moved there to avoid a painful existence and felt the need to come up with an identity that masked who they truly were, but that was something I had to deal with in New York, too. The fucked-up transplants in New York just seemed more genuine, though.

I was a New Yorker at heart, and would toil away until I was able to fly to LA for directing gigs on private jets. In reality, I knew I had a skewered vision and would probably be taking the F train to gigs the rest of my life.

Thanks to a friend, I landed an internship in the costume department of *SNL* and found myself working part time in the script department a few months later. That job turned full-time and before I knew it, my plan was falling into place! Unfortunately, this is where it almost ended. Years passed, and still I found myself proofing scripts. Although I submitted my writing each summer in the hopes of being hired as a writer, it never happened. Looking back, I realize this was because I was trying to write for performers I had nothing in common with. It took me years to realize my best writing (if I can even call it that?) comes from expressing my unique super-gay voice. While I worked on a host of outside projects to keep myself satisfied, I still had to proof those damn scripts for a living. To say the least, script coordinating is mind numbing. All you do is look for spelling errors and make sure there are two fucking spaces after each period.

To entertain myself after I grew bored, I decided to play a joke on my anal retentive supervisor, who would proof each and every page, ensuring no mistakes would enter the sacred script. Knowing she'd catch any error, I altered the famous line that opens the show each week. By some twist of fate, she looked for a change I made on a different page and sent the script to be duplicated. The next day, as I was flipping through my copy, I came across the last page of the opening sketch, which read:

DARRELL

Live from New York, work this pussy!!

My stomach dropped. I rushed over to my supervisor. I was sure I'd be fired. Especially since this sketch was written by a very esteemed writer who (ironically) did not have a sense of humor. Instead of being mad, she found the whole thing hilarious. The two of us ran to the Supervising Producer to tell him what happened. "Oh, thank God," he said. "I was waiting for a fight with the standards people! This makes everything easier." I revised the page and sent it out to everyone on staff.

Later that day, when the writer came to rehearse his piece, he was completely unaware his sketch was re-written by a bored Script Coordinator. But to this day, part of me wishes I never caught it in time, just to see the look on his face as "President Clinton" said, "Live from New York, Work This Pussy!" The fact that this is something I thought of writing in the first place only serves to remind me why I have yet to jet off to Los Angeles to shoot a film with Julianne Moore.

CHAPTER 5.

SORRY, DARLIN'

I used to think it would be so cool to run into a celebrity you loved and recite a line from one of their movies to them. So when I ran into Gina Gershon at an *SNL* after-after party one night, I seized my opportunity to say my favorite line from *Showgirls* while she poured a beer from the keg. With no introduction, I grabbed her hand, looked at her nails and said, "I'm not into that whore look, anymore, darlin'." What followed next can only be described as the most uncomfortable eight seconds of my life, as she looked around the room for security, turned, and walked away.

CHAPTER 6.

CYBIL

Like a moron, I thought the producers of *Saturday Night Live* might notice me as the "brilliant" writer/performer I was if I put on a one-man show during the summer following my first season working in the script department. The show I wrote, "Man-A-Thon" was about nine gay men who lived in the same apartment building in Chelsea – a surefire way to get me cast on a mainstream comedy show in 1997!! I originally called it "Fag-Fest," but even my most out-there friends thought that a bit much.

During Wednesday read-throughs, when everyone on staff crowded into a room to listen to the host and cast read through 40 sketches, I stayed at my desk, writing and re-writing the show. It was a perfect plan, since anyone passing by my desk thought I was formatting scripts. In reality, I was writing monologues for Jojo the club kid and Steven, the recovering alcoholic!

As the season progressed, I asked my high school friend John, a part-time theatre manager, to direct the show since he studied Drama at NYU. As it turned out, John had the directing instincts of a three-year old cat, and was more adept at watching theatre than creating it. That was fine by me. Since I was a fearless 25 year-old, I didn't need anyone to direct me! What could some outsider have to say about these people who lived in my head? So when John sat through rehearsals and said, "great" after each run-through, I believed him. He was just thrilled to be working in *the theatre*! I really shouldn't say anything bad about John, as he is still my friend – er – he did a good job? The same cannot be said for the lighting designer we hired, a brazen red head named Sally.

Sally was one of those people you only seem to meet in Off-Off Broadway theatres. A former actress, she became a techie after college, thinking it would be more lucrative than doing extra work on *As The World Turns*. Considering we paid her $50 a show, I highly doubt she made a killing in the world of Off-Off Broadway Lighting. She also happened to be obnoxious beyond belief, and spoke loudly and with intensity about absolutely *everything* in between drags of cigarettes. At one point, we thought of re-naming the show "Woman-A-Thon" and throwing Sally up there with a pack of her Lucky Strikes. That woman could talk.

Before each show, I was always too nervous to check in with her to see how things were looking. I was usually pacing backstage, hoping I wasn't about to have another case of the shits. Thankfully, that only happened once, right before I zipped myself into that silver cat suit to play Jojo, the club kid, who opened the show dressed in white kabuki makeup, a blonde Princess Leia wig with birds nesting in it and a giant see-through smiley-face backpack I wore backwards so I could access the drink tickets and ecstasy tabs Jojo carried around. As I strutted on stage to "Rave The Rhythm" – a techno song popular at Limelight's Disco 2000 – I made my way center stage and opened the show complaining about the state of NYC nightlife post-Giuliani:

> JOJO: Hello!! What the fuck am I supposed to do now? I just went to the Tunnel for the Albino Lesbian Styrofoam Party and it's been shut down! I'm all dressed up, waiting to pass the velvet ropes, and instead, there are police barricades up! The whole scene was so *Happy Days* meets *NYPD Blue*. Giuliani is shutting down all the clubs in New York! It's an outrage! I mean, what's a club kid to do? All dressed up, in my Princess Leia meets Pamela Lee wig, and nowhere to go. I'm so bummed; I'm calling it a night. Who am I fooling – I'm all wired from the E I just popped, there's no way I'm going to bed for at least another five hours. Uh, this sucks! Limelight's shut down, Michael Alig's in jail for chopping Angel up…Being a club kid is not as fabulous as it was two years ago…as if! Anyway, I used to live on Avenue A and tenth street, in a fifteen square foot studio. I had to share a bathroom with the entire floor, my shower was in the living room, and I had to share a kitchen with a Pakistani family whose favorite dish was curry eggs and goat's head. But I was living in New York. My rent there was only $1450 a month. Then I moved to DUMBO — you know, down under the Manhattan Bridge overpass? Then I moved to ASKAS — you know, across the street from King and Splash? Anyway, now I'm sharing this fierce studio in Chelsea. It's just like *Three's A Crowd*, but with two people. Oh my God, Chelsea, can you believe it? I never thought I'd go above 14th Street in my life, but then all the yuppies and people from Queens moved in. The East Village is sooo Rachel and Ross get their bellies pierced on *Friends*. Hello! Go to Hoboken! Leave me alone and let me get my scrotum pierced in peace!!!

After Jojo, I went through my litany of characters, including Steven, the recovering alcoholic; Val, a lounge singer from Atlantic City; Joe, the metal head superintendent; Frankie, a flaming jewelry designer based on my cousin of the same name; Miguel, a voguer from Jackson Heights; Chantelle Quatifa Laquan, a transsexual prostitute; and capped the show off with Chauncy Charleston, an over-the-top parody of a fashion writer. You know, typical *SNL* stuff.

It was a standard one-man show, with me changing behind a screen as a backlight illuminated me in silhouette. A song which captured whatever character was coming on next played as my dresser and I changed in a flurry. Somehow, I convinced my friend, Vincent to be the dresser, and each week, he showed up for the thankless task of helping me change into nine costumes. He did a great job, but later confessed he was frightened by the quick change that took place just before the transsexual prostitute went on. During that one, he had just ten seconds to get this tragic wig I made by gluing 14th Street hair extensions on a swim cap onto my head. To do it right, he had to stretch it real wide, or I'd wind up looking like Jocelyn Wildenstein. Without fail, he always got me back on stage before the 50 seconds John and I allotted for each change. Although most of the time I looked like I was recovering from a bad eye lift.

Vincent was a professional, but the same can't be said for that loudmouth, Sally. The first sign we might be having trouble with her came during Chantelle's first appearance, when I walked to the spot where she delivered her monologue and found myself in darkness. Thrown off, I started walking around the stage, searching for a spotlight...or any light. Since she was a prostitute, it was fine she worked the stage in the dark, so the audience had no idea she wasn't supposed to be in black the entire scene.

When the show was over, I asked Sally what happened. She told me, "a light must have blown" and she'd look into it. The next week, when I found Serene Steven giving his address to a room full of alcoholics in a candy-red, heart-shaped spotlight, I knew something was up. We soon discovered Sally was just using whatever lighting plan the 8:00 show had set up, hoping their cues would match with hers. Seventy percent of the time, she was right. But thirty percent of the time, I found myself in darkness or in green clover spotlights which had nothing to do with whatever character was on stage.

It also didn't help that the Kraine Theatre was located directly across the street from Bijou 82, a "theater" which was actually a gay sex club. Each week, our ticket agent would have to issue refunds to seedy men who accidentally wound up at the Kraine Theatre instead of the Bijou. And since their idea of a "Man-A-Thon" was slightly different from the version being performed by the loud queen on stage with multiple personality disorder, they would slither out during the first blackout and ask for a refund.

Beyond that, "Man-A-Thon" was a decent run. Thanks to my friend Jessica, who showed up drunk each week, I was guaranteed at least one person would be cackling, egging others on to laugh. I got a review in "HX" magazine that called my performance "chameleon-like," but I'm pretty sure that's just because we paid five hundred bucks to advertise in the theatre section.

As far as luring producers from *SNL*, the only person who came was my supervisor, who ran on stage while I was still dressed as Chauncey Charleston to say, "I think a lot of the people knew you because I didn't find it as funny as they did." This woman eventually went on to have children. Months later, this same woman told me I should check out a show one of the writers at the show put on. She said, "Now *that's* a one man show!"

Although I loved doing theatre, "Man-A-Thon" cost over $2,000 to produce, and I only made back a grand. The risks in theatre were too high, and so I decided that next summer, I would utilize my hiatus to write and direct a feature film that would only set me back $28,000.

CHAPTER 7.

A NEGLIGIBLE INDIE RELEASE

In June of 1998, I decided to write and direct a feature film called "Glam-Trash" even though my only writing and directing experience consisted of shooting two music videos in college and airing three talk show parodies on Manhattan Public Access. What can I say? I'm an Aries – the most naïve sign of the Zodiac. We're bold, yet sometimes, blind. Even before I started production on this insanely low budget film, I began to see life was starting to imitate art.

"Glam-Trash" is about a fashion designer who must overcome loads of obstacles to put on a runway show in a New York City nightclub. When shooting the film, everyone worked day and night to get it shot, even though we, too, faced ridiculous obstacles, monsoon-like storms, uppity extras and various struggles every step of the way. At the end of the film, the lead character, Jen speaks the following line that summed everything up about making the movie:

JEN
...Now that I think about it – who cares? We have all been born with the talent to do what we do – design, act,

perform, whatever – and I'll be damned if I let people who roam this earth, afraid of anything different affect what I do. You've just gotta keep doing it – come hell or high water, standing ovations or rotting fruit. 'Cause I'll be damned if I let some talentless, afraid-of-living loser tear me and my friends down!

Little did I know these words would come to haunt me for the rest of my life.

It all started three days before we started shooting, when I received a frantic call from Sylvia Wong, one of the Asian sweatshop workers, who told me she refused to shoot the film unless she had lines because she "doesn't do extra work." With only three Asian women lined up for the sweat shop scene which actually called for twenty, the only thing I could do was agree to write her a scene and fax it over for her approval.

A few minutes later, the cinematographer Chris, called to say he wouldn't be able to shoot the film because the D.P. he worked for was forcing him to take a job. He told me not to worry because he was hooking me up with "the most talented D.P." in NYC. Part freaked out, part relieved at the prospect of getting rid of this name-dropping, Michael Bolton look-alike, I agreed to meet his replacement. I mean, what the fuck else was I gonna do?

The next day, I laid eyes on Ted, a complete douchebag with a *ponytail* and B.O. that always brought to mind homeless people on the F train. All was well until he told me he needed an additional *ten thousand dollars* of equipment and a 14-foot truck to hold it all. I tried not to be scared when it dawned on me I would be driving this monstrosity to and from locations the whole shoot.

The very next day, I wound up driving that thing right into the side of the Williamsburg Bridge, ripping off the side view mirror during the first of a thousand monsoon-like thunderstorms. I continued driving to the apartment that served as our main location in Jackson Heights, blindly hoping each time I changed lanes I wasn't about to kill a small family.

When I finally arrived at the apartment, I threw my back out unloading all of the equipment Ted ordered with my best friend/therapist/art director for the next two weeks, Jen. As I lay on the couch waiting for the Advil to kick in, Jen informed me the truck had just received the first of what would turn out to be 12 parking tickets across the street.

At seven o'clock, I finally got to meet the script coordinator, Lila. A few minutes into our conversation, she told me she was actually a dominatrix. She had dropped by on her way to one of her slave's apartments for a "session" on 85th Street to say hello before we started the next day. It was all coming together?

On the first day of shooting, a rift developed between Ted and his pretentious two person crew and the ten friends who made up my crew. Every two seconds, he'd scream, "Art Department" even though he knew the art department was Jen, who must lower pictures, paintings and vases every time he reframed a shot. While doing this, he'd talk about film in the most pretentious way, while I was trying to shoot a *movie* I was hoping might come off as a tribute to my idol, John Waters. Thanks to his lumbering style, we started running really behind schedule. Each day, I had to rewrite scenes on the fly so the film would at least make sense. This continued until three AM, when we finally wrapped our *first day?!?!*

Chaos and calamity ensued for the next two weeks. In that time, I dropped twelve pounds; managed to wrangle

Michael Musto and Jaid Barrymoore into shooting cameos; passed out from dehydration while shooting in an apartment that was so hot, pictures started sliding down the walls; recast five roles on the set when actors didn't show up; pay a nightclub a $2000 location fee on my maxed-out VISA; somehow fill that club with seventy extras; make a drag queen's dress out of a tablecloth; almost get arrested for peeing on the sidewalk; find out Jen has secretly broken down in the bodega four times; the grip has been smoking pot and possibly crack in the truck, and the dominatrix and the gaffer have started having an affair. But *somehow*, we wrapped on schedule a week and a half later.

When all was said and done, "Glam-Trash" somehow got through post-production and became an actual movie that got picked up by a distributor. A distributor who ran away with every dime the movie made, setting me back $28,000. They told me they weren't able to sell the movie to any video stores, but three years later, thousands of VHS tapes wound up on eBay with Blockbuster stamps on them. This was also around the time I found out the movie was available to download for free on some Russian website.

Although it was supposed to run 90 minutes, "Glam-Trash" wound up being just 65 minutes long because I had to rewrite so many scenes in the hopes an actual story would be told. Looking back, the film has all the flaws of a first-time writer/director working with no budget: horrible acting and directing, poor sound design and a script that could have used a lot more rewrites. But after everything I went through, I was happy to just have *something* to show for it. Even if it was a film *Time Out New York* called "a negligible indie release" that would be best

enjoyed "if you had a drink first." Hey, it could be worse.
At least they said it could be "enjoyed," right?

The VHS box designed by those dirtbags over at Canis Lupus Entertainment

CHAPTER 8.

IN THE BEGINNING...

Why are parents disappointed when their children grow up to be gay, mentally ill or alcoholic? I mean, take a look at your gene pool: Uncle Gary and his "special friend" own an antique shop, Aunt Phyllis has the nerves and Grandpa Harry's been carrying around that flask since 1977. So just who did you expect to pop out of your vagina? Eleanor Roosevelt?

The first clue: My mother totally should have known I was gay when I told her I wanted to be Wonder Woman for Halloween when I was five years old. But still, this woman was shocked when I came out fourteen years and countless costumes later...

The second clue: My father totally should have known I was gay, when, on the first day of Little League, I placed my mitt up to my face to catch a ball, and wound up hobbling around the field with a black eye and a broken pair of glasses. But still, this man was shocked when I came out seven years and countless black eyes later.

The third clue: I'm not even gonna mention those white capezios.

CHAPTER 9.

MINT IN BOX

Why did the nerds have to ruin *Star Wars*? As a child, I loved the *Star Wars* films. I collected all the toys and kept each and every one in great shape. To this day, I still have every action figure released from the first three movies and two boxes of play sets and spaceships, including The Millennium Falcon, The Death Star and Wampa – a Yeti-like creature from *The Empire Strikes Back*. I even have a ceramic R2D2 bank my mother made me for my ninth birthday. The only problem is, I never tell anyone this because the nerds ruined *Star Wars* back in 1990. It was right around the time George Lucas started whoring out *The Star Wars Trilogy* by re-releasing the films with fifteen seconds of "digitally enhanced" footage and added "scenes," like Jabba The Hut "walking" through a shot which looked like it was scribbled on the film cells with a wax marker. That's around the time I started realizing my childhood fantasy had turned into a nightmare.

I should have seen the writing on the wall in third grade, when John Fitzgerald and his weirdo friends used to play games based on the movies during recess at PS133 while the rest of us played tag or fell to our deaths from the monkey bars. John and the rest of the nerds would run around pretending to be Cloud Car Pilots or other obscure characters most people didn't even know were *in* the movies. Except me, who knew what they were up to because I had both the Asian *and* Black Cloud Car Pilots in my C-3PO case back home, sandwiched right between Princess Leia and Chief Chirpa.

Now that I'm a fully-grown and reasonably well-adjusted adult, there is no way I can admit to owning any of these toys. To do so might lead people to believe I'm one of those freaks with a Darth Vader phone in his bedroom right next to his stack of porn mags and week-old Chinese take-out containers. And since I don't want to take the chance of someone thinking I was one of those losers who camped out to see *Episode Three*, the toys sit in my grandmother's attic, where they have collected dust since 1986.

Every once in a while, I'll take them out and remember all the fun I used to have with them as a kid. I'll think of the time I stole the light saber out of Mike Regan's Luke Skywalker figure after I lost mine, or how my mother used a toothpick to put Princess Leia's head back on after Jorge Gonzalez ripped it off with his teeth. Or that C-3PO figure I had that turned white after I dropped him in a mug of hot chocolate. I know I can probably make a fortune selling them on eBay, but part of me just doesn't want to get rid of them. The nerd part.

CHAPTER 10.

ZIPPIDY-DOO-DA

One summer when I was fourteen, I was swimming in the above-ground pool in my parent's backyard in Bellerose, Queens when I felt the sudden urge to pee. Since my mother had a sign on the deck that read, "We don't swim in your toilet, please don't pee in our pool," I had no choice but to get out of the pool to use the bathroom. After I was finished, I quickly zipped up my bathing suit and...SNAGGED MY PENIS IN THE ZIPPER! Oh, the horror! Oh, the pain! I tried pulling the zipper back down, but it caught the skin! I tried pulling the zipper further up, but...THAT WAS THE DUMBEST IDEA I EVER DID HAVE! I tried jiggling my bathing suit, but that damn zipper just wouldn't budge! Seconds felt like minutes felt like hours. And my sopping bathing suit was weighing the whole thing down, pulling on my poor willy all the while!

Finally, I got the idea to hobble over to the medicine cabinet for a pair of scissors. I cut the bathing suit off around the zipper, so only it was attached to my member. That was a lot better. BUT THERE WAS STILL A ZIPPER ATTACHED TO MY PENIS! I finally got the brilliant idea to use tweezers to pry the zipper open. After several failed attempts, I was able to release my bloody shaft from the zipper. (Don't ask me why my bathing suit even *had* a zipper. This was the 80s.)

So I guess the moral of this story is: Pee in the pool.

CHAPTER 11.

MARCHING ORDERS

I've always been drawn to music, so when I first entered Saint Francis Prep high school in Fresh Meadows, Queens, I decided to join the band. Back in 1986, I was even more naïve than I am today and had no idea that band was filled with rejects, losers and brass instruments. In my mind, I was going to learn how to play the keytar and start a band like The B-52's! (FYI, this is a recurring theme in my life. I always start something thinking it's going to be amazing, only to wind up railing against its existence like three months later.)

When I discovered there were no keytars or synthesizers in the school band, I had to figure out what lame instrument I'd play. I decided on the baritone horn because our teacher, Mrs. Calloway told us whoever played that or the tuba could bring one home to practice with so they wouldn't have to lug an instrument around, labeling themselves a dork for all the world to see.

My friend John chose the tuba for the same reason, but our soon-to-be bestie, Georgia decided to play the saxophone because she apparently went to a few too many ska concerts. Even though the three of us were in completely different sections of the band, we somehow managed to sit next to one other at the ungodly 7:30AM band practices we had to attend. Once in class, we'd talk about whatever song won "Screamer of The Week" on our local new wave station, WLIR, while the rest of the band actually rehearsed.

Since John and I would not be caught dead carrying a tuba or a baritone horn on the Q76 bus, we never practiced. And since Georgia's idea of practicing the saxophone meant dancing in her bedroom while listening to Fishbone, the three of us were continually singled out for sucking. Well, at least John and I were. Half the time, Georgia wasn't even there, but no one knew because I always marked her present on the attendance sheet they passed around. The one time Mrs. Calloway got suspicious, Georgia was sent to the dean, and told his secretary, Barbara, she was there.

A few months into the school year, Mrs. Calloway decided to play a film that was supposed to entice everyone to join the most pathetic organization known to high schools across the nation besides the French Club–Marching Band. As the movie showed a bunch of nerds talking about "team spirit" and "how much they loved to inspire the football team," John, Georgia and I sat in our made-up section of the band making throw up sounds and laughing at its lameness.

As soon as Mrs. Calloway figured out we were the assholes subverting the film she was hoping would inspire everyone to join up, she sent us to the dean. On the way out the door, she pulled me aside and said, "You know, you've changed...and not for the better" – which totally made me feel like I was on *Knot's Landing* – probably not the reaction she was hoping for.

Somehow, we all passed that year, save for Georgia. When the three of us went to the music room to see what grades we got at the end of the semester, there was a huge asterisk next to her name. Our eyes trailed to the bottom of the page, and right next to the asterisk was a note:

*TOLD BARBARA SHE WAS THERE. INVESTIGATION PENDING.

When the Dean and Mrs. Calloway called Georgia in to perform one of the songs we had been playing all year, the stale fart that passed through her saxophone was all the evidence they needed to figure out she hadn't picked that thing up all year long.

CHAPTER 12.

SEX ED

In 1988, my high school held a bizarre 24-hour fundraiser called the Superdance to raise money for Muscular Dystrophy. Even as a 14 year old, the irony of having people dance for 24 hours for those who couldn't was not lost on me. The dance took place in the gymnasium, and every year, 2,000 students had to raise hundreds of dollars to attend. Over the course of the dance, there were breaks for meals and one three-hour sleep session, but beyond that, you were just supposed to dance. The more I think about it, the Superdance was like the first Circuit Party...with nuns.

Everything seemed innocent enough, until 3 A.M., when the lights were turned down and everyone took to their sleeping bags. A few sisters patrolled the floor, making sure no monkey business was going on, but that didn't stop my friends Georgia and Rebecca from deciding they were going to practice giving blowjobs on me. It didn't help matters that Rebecca starting going down on me while I was sleeping.

I felt strange, yet excited, as my first public sexual encounter started heating up. I looked around to see if anyone knew what was going on, and to my horror, saw Sister Joseph Agnes walking right towards us! She was making the rounds, and was currently over by the band nerds. At that moment, I realized the thrill of public sex came from thinking you might get caught. And I liked it.

I tapped Rebecca on the head and made a slashing throat move, and she got with the game plan immediately. The Sister passed right by us without noticing someone had their mouth clamped around my dick.

Rebecca re-emerged from the sleeping bag and in a flash, Georgia took her place. She started giving me head, and I realized neither of these girls needed practice. They were both amazing! But I wasn't about to stop them from polishing their skills. Just when I thought it couldn't get any better, Rebecca ducked into the sleeping bag and joined Georgia! That was it. I couldn't hold out any longer. I whispered to Rebecca I was about to come and like a seasoned pro, she started going down on me with more vigor. Ten seconds later, I was stifling my groans which seemed to arouse the curiosity of Sister Joseph Agnes, who was once again a few yards away.

I popped up in my sleeping bag, let out a moan and pretended I just woke up from a nightmare. Georgia and Rebecca slithered back to their sleeping bags as I distracted the nun by pretending I didn't know where I was.

"What's going on over there?" Sister Joseph Agnes whispered as she made her way through the sleeping masses.

"I had a nightmare," I said. She placed her hand on my forehead. "Poor dear, you're all sweated up. Do you want to see the nurse?" she asked.

"No, I'll be okay. I just want to get back to sleep," I said.

"You do that, lamb," she said as she stroked my hair. When she walked away, I looked over at Rebecca and Georgia, who were both chuckling. I thought about practicing my cunnilingus skills on them, but thought better of it.

Thus began my career as the "Annie, Annie, are you okay?" blowjob doll. I make reference to that mouth-to-mouth mannequin from health class because my dick would have just as many lips on it as Annie's mouth by the time I graduated high school. And just like Annie, I would feel used and abused as random people put their mouths on me so they could learn an important skill. In all honesty, these people weren't random. They were friends of mine, part of what people referred to as "my harem." That harem consisted of six girls, who would have been called "fag hags" if any of us had any clue what college had in store for us. We were great friends, and for that reason, these girls had no problem asking if they could practice oral sex on me.

Blowjob 101 happened in a lot of different places: the back of cars, the costume room after rehearsal for "Ten Little Indians" – you name it. These girls needed to feel they were skilled before they tried it out on a *real* guy, so who better to practice on than their closet-case friend? Since I was still confused about my sexuality, I practiced giving them oral sex, too. But after going down on two of them, I decided I would wait until a girlfriend made me do that. Thankfully, she never showed up.

CHAPTER 13.

GURL, PLEASE

In my freshman year of high school, I became a member of The Alvernian Drama Society, easily the most pretentious-sounding name of a theater club in the history of mankind. Each fall, we'd produce a play, and every spring, a musical. In one of our fall selections, a British farce called "See How They Run," I was cast as The Bishop of Lax, and must have subconsciously chosen to play this character as a raging queen because three of our school's brothers left in the first act because they thought I was ridiculing priests. The sad thing is I wasn't even aware I was doing this. I was just doing what came naturally.

Another sign I might one day become a flaming homo came during the run of "Ten Little Indians," when I decided to put on a see-through purple negligee one of the actresses wore. Much to the delight of my fellow closet-case actors and a few girls who inexplicably still had a crush on me, I ran up and down Francis Lewis Boulevard, holding a poster for the show while screaming at passing cars, "Come See The Play!"

Amazingly, half these people were surprised when I came out in college three years later. The other half laughed while asking things like, "You *really* didn't know?" and "This is for real?" Considering I was wearing hot pants and a lycra T-shirt at Limelight's Disco 2000 when I told them, I really can't blame them for their reaction.

CHAPTER 14.

I HOPE MY MOTHER DOESN'T READ THIS

The following are unaltered diary entries from my freshman year in college, when I was still shockingly confused about my sexual orientation?

April 7, 1990: Oh, dear. I've gotten myself into quite a mess. My scene is due in theatre class tomorrow and I've got no partner and I haven't gotten my lines down yet. Tomorrow is my 18th birthday, but I feel really depressed. I don't know why. What to do, what to do. I need a new job, I need self-confidence, I need a girlfriend, but most of all, I need a new haircut. I can't believe I'll be an 18 year old virgin. I never thought I would hate my life so much when I was younger. By the way, that fungus on my hip will be determined on the 14th at the Doctor's. I hope that I do not have AIDS. Maybe it's herpes. Oh well. Enough self pity.

May 5, 1990: Yesterday was the big black velour coat fiasco with Mom and Dad. I needed to get some blazers to wear for my new job at Macy's Herald Square, and I found this really great black velour suit jacket that looked totally 70's. Well, when I got it home and showed it to everyone, they all laughed and told me I looked like a pimp! Madonna's movie comes out on Friday. I still wish my face acne, back acne, chest acne and that fungus on my hip would go away.

I also can't wait to lose my virginity. I should have stood with Rebecca, Jen or Margaret long enough to – what I loser I was. I always seem to break up with my girlfriends after a month. I can't wait to see "Phantom of the Opera" on June 17th! Anyway, I feel better than last time I wrote. Goodnight.

June 4, 1990: I'm sitting in McDonald's drinking vodka while waiting to get picked up by David to go to Disco 2000 – should be fun. I just went downstairs to get some ice. I can't stand drinking warm alcohol. It's completely vulgar. Now onto the important thing. I'm beginning to think I might be...gay. There, I said it. But me being a chronic denyer, I can't face up to the facts. As Mariah Carey sang, "Someday." Well I'm gonna go now. Oh, but one more extremely important thing. I'm not even sure if I am gay. What I most enjoy is getting my dick sucked. In other words, I enjoy getting pleasure from men, and thus accordingly why not from women? It's so much easier to find a willing guy that maybe I just use guys as a way to get what I really want from a girl. Confusion. Am I straight or am I gay? Oh God, what kind of life am I headed for? A loveless, Godless, solitary existence? Is that all I'm worth? What a pitiful rollercoaster of a life I lead. Up and down. Oh well, in the immortal words of The Smiths, "Accept Yourself."

June 5, 1990: Last night was the whole Disco 2000 fiasco. David had to ruin it all. Who goes out without ID and dresses in jeans and a purple Champion sweatshirt to get into The Limelight!? Kenny Kenny let me right in with my hot shorts on. I'm feeling really horny lately and I think it's time I start to be totally honest here – I think I'm gonna drive to Cunningham Park for gay sex again. I'm in the mood for a blowjob. But all those guys are 30 year old losers. I want a hot 22 year old! I always vow to never go there again, but then, WHAMMO! There I am again with my pants down around my ankles getting blown by some loser with a bald spot and a baby seat in the back of his car.

June 14, 1990: Last night was the ultimate club trip at Disco 2000. I went with Jenny, John and Rachel. I went into the Lick It! Lounge for an hour and there were all these hot men fooling around. I got two hand jobs – one freaky guy and one dumpy one. Then I met this hot guy named Doug and we fooled around for twenty minutes on the radiator! When I finally got back to the straight part, Rachel and Jenny were freaking out, saying they couldn't find me anywhere! I just told them Lahoma Van Zandt got me into the VIP area.

July 20, 1990: Well, last night I left the Limelight with Doug. We fooled around in his bed and we did everything – and I mean everything. I must say, never again! I feel extremely guilty, confused, paranoid, and upset because of it. I enjoyed it a lot but is this what I want to be? Well, Doug is bi and as we laid in bed naked together, we discussed why we like girls. He slept with two girls from the Limelight and that totally made me jealous! I've vowed to lose my real virginity this summer at the latest. I'm gonna assert myself on every girl whenever I get a chance. It's my fuckin' life right? Why not grab life by the balls? (No pun intended.)

Aug. 1, 1990: What a night Friday was! Me, Jenny, Rachel, John and David went to The Building. I tried acid – it was fake. And then I tried coke – it was not! I had three lines and John had one. John and I had the best conversation – we talked for hours and then we went to the diner and talked some more. It was one of the best nights I've had in a while. Oh, Doug was there – he called me twice on Saturday. Get a life! Loser.

Aug. 15, 1990: On the way home from the Building, Jessica and Georgia gave me blowjobs and handjobs in the back seat. I didn't come again. Anyway, I'm gonna tell them they can't practice on me anymore. On a brighter note, I plan on working out again. And varoom – watch out – Musclemania! Then I'll be able to pick up everyone I want without feeling self-conscious – if only I could lick this premature ejaculation thing.

Aug. 30, 1990: I am so elated. I'm flaming and I know it. I can't wait to tell everyone about it. (But I must.) Life is great, but life sucks.

CHAPTER 15.

IM EXCLUSIVE

Back in the 80s and 90s, there was a catalog called "International Male" which had the magical ability to locate every single gay teenager in the United States. How did they do this? Did they scour the drama clubs of every high school? Send out scouts to see who wore white capezios to gym class? Whatever dark arts they utilized, every gay man I know has received a copy of this catalog at some point in their formative years.

I call it a catalog, but I don't know anyone who has ever admitted to actually ordering from it. That's because the "clothing" they carried consisted of the most outrageous collection of "fashion" no self-respecting gay man would ever be caught dead in. If you could imagine what Little Richard might wear to a sex party at Siegfried and Roy's mansion, you might get an idea of how over-the-top their ensembles were. To make matters worse, most of the clothes were made from polyester, nylon, and various other "fabrics" that ended in the term "-like" or "-esque."

Here are some of my favorites:

1. A gold lamé *pant suit*.

2. A ten button "Officer's Suit" with a jacket that came just below the knees.
3. A striped, purple, satin-esque "top" (their words) with banded collar.
4. A pink, calf-length, seven button jacket with matching shirt, pants, and tie.
5. A belted, turquoise square-cut swimsuit that looked like a castaway from the design sessions of the original "Wonder Woman."

I always made sure to check the sale pages when the catalog arrived because they always featured the most outrageous clothes even tacky "International Male" customers wouldn't buy. Like that velour suit that came with a matching cape, or the crushed velvet, mock turtleneck, short sleeve tank, available in lavender and lime green.

Half the catalog was filled with these kinds of clothes, but the other half featured underwear one would not be able to find anywhere else. Items like "The Sock" – a jock-like device that wrapped around one's manhood without any straps. Or rows and rows of mesh underwear in every color of the rainbow. There was also a man-girdle that came in two pieces – one to strap the fat around your gut in with, and another to keep your man-tits wrapped closely to your chest. It seemed people who wore loud, tacky clothes were also on the robust side.

Although the clothing in "International Male" was comical, the men were seriously drop-dead gorgeous. They were always perfect male specimens with five percent body fat and lean, ripped bodies. And when they combined the duo of gorgeous men + skimpy underwear,

"International Male" scored big time. In fact, the only reason anyone ever looked at the catalog was so they could check out the package on that hot guy in the Greek Bikini swimsuit or the Pocket Thong. As if the thongs weren't revealing enough, they also included close-ups so one could make out the contour of their hefty packages, which had no doubt been fluffed before the shoot.

For this reason, "International Male" was jerk-off material for gay teens across the nation. Every single one of us were thrilled when we discovered pages of gorgeous men in Varsity Rower Shorts and Pouch Thongs in our mailbox!

In order to make sure I would continue to receive this jack-fest, I broke the Silent Code of Self-Respecting Gays and ordered something from it when I was seventeen. Since I had no money because I was working at a local drug store chain called Genovese two days a week, I had just enough money to buy a $7 faux-leather bracelet with copper trimmings I found on the sale page.

When I phoned up IM – as us insiders called it – a surly queen answered the phone. After I told him I would like to order the Mandalay Bay Bracelet, he snapped, "And..."

"And...that's it," I said.

"You mean to tell me you're willing to pay $5.50 in shipping for a $7 bracelet, bringing your grand total to $12.50," he said. I guess my order was a lot skimpier than his last client, who probably bought a Chartreuse Melton Wool Shawl Collar Jacket and a Red Velvet Holiday Suit in XXL.

"Uh, yeah, that's it," I stuttered. This was my first time dealing with a self-hating homosexual and I was thrown.

"Thank you for ordering from International Male. My name is Jeffrey and it has been a *real* pleasure serving you," he said. Something told me he added that *"real"* into his script. I hung up and awaited my Mandalay Bay Bracelet, which would ensure "IM" would be stuffed in my mailbox for years to come.

Boy, was I right. Five residences and twenty-three years later, I still receive this catalog – which has now morphed into the "Undergear" catalog. To be honest, I always love when it comes, because I can show it to my friends and say, "I was thinking of getting this white and black striped knee-length three-piece suit for Sharon's wedding." The look on their faces always makes up for the fact that my mailman probably thinks I ordered from this catalog…which I did…but does that purple, lace-up square cut swimsuit with matching cape really count?

CHAPTER 16.

THE OLD IN AND OUT

In fashion, they say what goes around, comes around, and as I get older, I find this to be true. Styles come and go over and over again, but with slight variations. Right now, there's a hairstyle men have been rocking called The Top Ponytail. If it doesn't ring a bell, it's when a man has long hair he pulls into a bun on the top of his head. It's been going strong for a while now, which can only mean it's about to run it's course. And if it ever comes back again, I will murder someone.

On a related note, in 1985, there was a two-tone style of jeans girls wore I kept praying to Jesus they'd make for boys. The front of the jeans were black, and the back, grey. Or the back would be blue, and the front, black. God, I just loved those jeans. But they didn't make them for boys. So fashion stylists, if you're reading this, please bring them back, cuz I totally have the balls to wear them now.

Whatever you do, do *not* bring back acid wash jeans. *Ever.*

CHAPTER 17.

GANDU-GANDU

Don't buy porn in your neighborhood unless you want everyone knowing your business. When I was in college, I used to buy "Manshots" at Optimo, a local smoke shop on Hillside Avenue. It was owned by "the Indian" and I would shop there because I figured no one else would step foot inside his store, since my entire hometown of Bellerose was filled with predominantly white, middle class racists. Little did I know, but "the Indian" would soon drop his cigarette prices below that of the 7-11 next door and the whole town would start clamoring to get inside.

As fate would have it, "the Indian" would soon fall in love with my sister, Diane, for the simple reason that she was the only person in Bellerose who treated him like a human being. Whenever she'd come in for a pack of Marlboro Lights, she'd ask how his day was, warn him about impending blizzards, and comment on his beard. He'd respond by giggling like a fourteen year-old girl, and often send her into the night without charging her. Somehow, Raja, as we learned his name to be, got our phone number, and started calling to ask her out on dates. My father was taken aback the first time he heard a forty-year old Indian man calling to speak with his teenage daughter, but soon got used to his nightly calls. Nothing came from his advances, and soon Raja moved to West Virginia to torment the hillbilly racists of the South. It was around this time we found out Raja had a wife and *seven children* back in India.

A month after I stopped shopping at Optimo because I was afraid of running into Mrs. Delvechio with a copy of "Inches" in my hands, my best friend, Sergio, went in to buy a forty. When Raja handed him his change, he leaned over the counter and said, "So Diane's brother is gandu-gandu, eh?"

When Sergio asked what the hell "gandu-gandu" meant, he replied, in a hushed voice, "gay." Since Sergio knew I was gay for about a year (or probably eight if he had half a brain), I figured it wasn't a big deal...until everyone in Bellerose started calling me "Gandu Gandu."

In years to come, this meddling shop owner would have the last laugh on the homophobic racists of Bellerose, too. If you drive down Hillside Avenue today, you will see curried goat and incense for sale in all of the shop windows, as thousands of Indians have displaced the bigoted Irish and Italian families who once called Bellerose their home. My question is, where do they go to buy their porn?

Like anyone has to go anywhere to find porn these days. Nowadays, all a teenager has to do is type "boobies" on the iPhone, iPad and Powerbook his parents bought him when he was three to bring up five million pictures and videos. These devices have also turned everyone into amateur porn stars – texting, SnapChatting and posting nude selfies and pictures of their junk for all the world to see.

And thanks to sites like Tumblr, we have access to porn on our phones with just two swipes. There are downsides to this, though. Recently, I decided to scroll through Tumblr before going to bed one night. After coming across a stimulating video and doing my business, I clicked out of the app and turned in. Eight hours later, I awoke to *nine* texts from Verizon, telling me I had burned through 8 gigs of data! Apparently, the video was playing on a loop while my wifi was down, costing me ninety dollars and making me pine for the days when I could buy a two pack of "Inches" and "Black Inches" for just ten bucks.

I called up Verizon to see if there was anything they could do. For once, I got a nice woman on the phone, and not that gruff Midwestern man who never has any time for me. Realizing I wouldn't get far if I told her the truth, I altered the story by saying one of my friends texted me a link to a Golden Girls video – which is totally something one of my gaylord friends would do.

"You're never gonna believe this," I told her. "I was heading to bed when a friend sent me a link to a 'The Golden Girls' clip. I thought it stopped playing, but apparently it was on a loop! I had no idea!"

She replied, "Oh, I just love 'The Golden Girls'! Let me see what I can do." A few minutes later, she came back and told me she was able to take eighty dollars off my bill. So lady at Verizon, if you're reading this, I just want to say, "Thank you for being a friend." And if you have the ability to research what I *really* watched that night...don't. Just don't.

CHAPTER 18.

LET'S ROCK!

In 1990, I became obsessed with the ABC series, *Twin Peaks*. Besides being a huge David Lynch fan, I was drawn to this quirky nighttime soap because I had never seen anything like it on TV before. All the characters and storylines were surreal and bizarre, two traits usually linked to Lynch, but never to network TV. Some people loved Leland Palmer or the Log Lady, but for me, the best character was the midget from the dream sequence. Now, I know the term "midget" is politically incorrect, but back in 1990, no one referred to him as the "little person" from *Twin Peaks*, so shut it.

For a full year, I replayed the scene where this height-challenged man, played by Michael J. Anderson, spoke backwards while dancing in a red-curtained room. Friends knew that whenever they came over, they would have to sit through this scene as I sat on the couch in my parent's paneled basement, repeating, "I've got good news. That gum you like is going to come back in style!" It was easily the best sequence on television, ever.

As fate would have it, Michael started making appearances at New York nightclubs at the height of the show's fame. I found out from Michael Musto's column in *The Village Voice* that he was slated to appear at The Building one Friday night. The club, located in an old warehouse in Chelsea, was large and cavernous, but had just one VIP lounge. I knew finding him would not be difficult.

The night of his appearance, I got to the club around midnight and started my search. I checked the VIP lounge, the dance floor and each and every bar, but he was nowhere to be found. Around two AM, I asked a few of the bartenders if "the midget from *Twin Peaks* was there," only to have them stare at me like I was speaking Indonesian. Apparently, the rest of the world did not share my latest obsession.

An hour later, I made my way back to the VIP lounge for one last look. As I passed the velvet ropes, I scanned the room and saw...Michael J. Anderson sitting on one of the couches! I ran over to introduce myself, and within seconds, he whipped out a joint.

"You wanna get high?" he asked. I could not believe what was happening. I was about to get high with the midget from *Twin Peaks*.

We shared a joint and I told him how much I loved him. "You are my favorite character to ever appear on television, with the obvious exception of Rerun from *What's Happening*!!" I told him.

"Well, I'm glad to know I'm in such esteemed company," he replied.

I asked him to autograph a picture I had taken of him off the TV, and he readily agreed. He grabbed it and wrote, "To Greg, There's always music in the air! – Little Mike." I pocketed the picture and excused myself, thanking him profusely. To this day, I have yet to have a more exciting celebrity encounter, and I doubt I ever will.

Sure, I meet celebrities and musicians every week at "SNL" but now I'm jaded and could care less. The last time I had a thrilling encounter was when Lady Gaga was the musical guest back in 2009. On the day of the show, she decided to change one of the songs she was performing, and I had to go into her dressing room to talk about what she would be doing so I could relay the information to the director, who would be shooting her performance sight unseen.

After telling me what song she would be singing and describing the choreography, she took one look at the lightning bolt pendant I wore around my neck, turned to her manager and said, "It's going to be all right! He has a lightning bolt! The universe is on our side!" At that moment, I realized Lady Gaga was a straight-up Aries flake like I was, gave her a big smile and told her it would indeed be all right.

Celebrities. They're just like us!

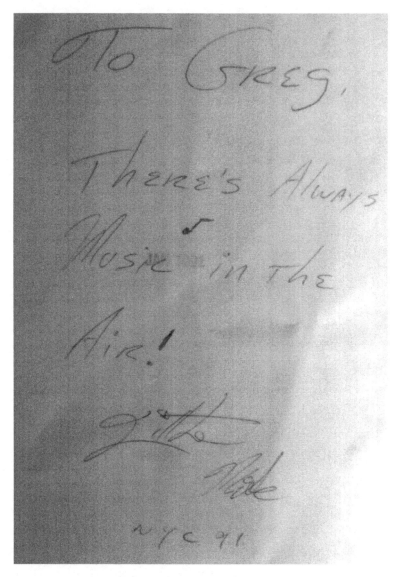

The back of the picture Michael J. Anderson signed for me

CHAPTER 19.

DEEPER AND DEEPER

I was really influenced by Madonna's "Erotica" album. Some might label me the Gayest Person Of The Millennium for saying this, but I am willing to take that risk. "Erotica" came out in 1992, just when I stopped telling my friends I was "bisexual" and admitted I was actually a big old homo, and it became the soundtrack to my coming out era. "Erotica" was released during my freshmen year in college, and I listened to it while commuting on the F train, reading Michael Musto's "La Dolce Musto" in *The Village Voice* and while getting ready to go out at night. I can distinctly remember listening to "Deeper and Deeper" while tweezing my eyebrows before I went to Sound Factory Bar on West 21st Street – a grooming phase that thankfully passed.

As I threw on my favorite white and black-striped lycra shirt and spritzed myself with Joop! cologne (another phase that thankfully passed), I'd sashay out of my room and tell my mother I was going to Sullivan's, a straight bar in Bayside, Queens. Then I'd hop on the F train and head over to my friend, Charles' apartment in Sheridan Square. We'd drop a hit of X (this was before it was called "E" or

"Molly" or whatever the fuck the kids call it today) and go dancing. Five hours later, we'd head back to his apartment as the sun came up, sharing painful stories about gym class while "Bad Girl" played in the background.

Produced by Shep Pettibone, "Erotica" is easily Madonna's best dance album besides her debut and "Confessions On A Dance Floor," which was made for that express purpose. I hate to use the word "dance" because so many people confuse it with hideous music, like that song, "Be My Lover" by Labouche or most things labeled "Freestyle." There are many types of dance music, and when it's done tastefully, it's amazing, and when it's not, it's painful, like EDM. Sorry, Skrillex.

"Erotica" falls in the former category. From the opening bass line that starts off the album, you just know it's gonna be a great ride. A lot of critics say it's her worst album because it only sold like two million copies, but how bad can an album be when they release six singles and four of them are top twenty hits? First came "Erotica," "Deeper & Deeper," "Rain," "Fever," "Bad Girl" and finally, "Bye Bye Baby." Now when was the last time an album had six singles? Nowadays, an artist is lucky to get one song released before the album falls from the charts. But "Erotica" had *six* singles.

Although I enjoyed "Bad Girl," mainly because of the music video starring Christopher Walken, I always found the lyrics ridiculous: "Bad girl, drunk by six, kissing someone else's lips. Smoked too many cigarettes today…not happy this way." So what, you got drunk and smoked a few cigarettes? Things could be a lot worse. Look at some other celebrities at the time. A bad day for Courtney Love would have consisted of shooting a speedball, stabbing your best friend and running over an infant on the way to AA.

Shep Pettibone, who had been producing great dance music since the 80s, decided to go with an underground house sound for the album. Critics called it "sleaze" but I called it heaven. Especially the remixes, which turned the sleaze up a notch. As a 19-year-old emerging homosexual, these songs were the perfect soundtrack to the debaucherous existence I was just starting to lead.

Madonna released "Erotica" along with the highly-derided *Sex* book. Critics and common folk said it was a piece of crap because it fell apart after the second viewing, but no one mentioned what was inside those poorly wired silver covers: Nude pictures of *Madonna* having sex with just about *everybody*. I mean, where else were you going to see Madonna licking Tony Ward's ass? That alone was worth the 50 bucks. And that spread with Naomi Campbell and Big Daddy Kane? And don't even get me started on that photo of Madonna wearing that long weave and crouching like an animal on the beach.

The only thing I hated about *Sex* were the ridiculous "stories" she wrote for it. Ones that started with sentences such as, "I like my pussy. Sometimes I stare at it in the mirror." But *Sex* is not about this nonsense. It's about the pictures. Super-hot photo shoots at locations like The Gaiety Male Burlesque with porn star Joey Stefano being led around on a leash. Or that S&M shoot that took place at The Vault. Now that one really got my attention.

I always wanted to go to The Vault because years before it was a sex club, it was a nightclub called Mars. In the late 80s and early 90s, Mars was one of the best clubs in NYC, along with Red Zone and MK. It was located in the heart of the meat packing district – which at the time, was filled with transsexual prostitutes that used to work those cobblestone streets in latex boots that reached just below the surprise between their thighs. Many nights, they would beckon to me as I walked to the club with my friend, Rachel Magnuson.

I was attracted to Rachel the minute I saw her in the back of the Q43 bus. Why? Because she was insane. I've always been attracted to lunatics, and she was certifiable. She was the first girl at Saint Francis Prep to wear fishnet stockings under her uniform skirt, dye her hair purple hair and wear matching lipstick. There was a funereal air about her, and like a "Fly On The Windscreen," I was attracted to it. What amazed me most about Rachel was the fact that she lived in Bellerose. For fifteen years, I thought I was the only freak living in that wasteland of mediocrity. So when I found out we were both listening to Morrissey's "Viva Hate" on the way to school one day, we became instant friends.

Rachel lived with her grandmother because she hated her mother and one day just decided she was moving in with her. This woman had no idea what hit her when Rachel showed up on her front stoop in a Depeche Mode T-shirt and a suitcase in her hand. I'm sure the last thing this 76 year-old wanted was the onslaught of chaos Rachel brought into her life in her golden years. All she wanted to do was drive her rust-colored Cadillac to church while worrying about the horrors of *rain!!!* and *gas prices!!!* But thanks to Rachel, she was worrying about whether her granddaughter was getting expelled for showing up to Religion 101 drunk again. I'm still amazed this woman didn't drop dead that time I called her at 4 AM to tell her Rachel was arrested for kicking someone in the face at Limelight.

Thinking it was 1962, her grandmother would banish her to the bedroom as punishment. But that didn't stop Rachel from sneaking out of the house whenever she felt like it. At ten o'clock, I'd creep into her backyard and tap on her bedroom window. Minutes later, she'd climb down my back in whatever crazy outfit she threw together as she hit her dog, Koko, in the head to stop him from barking.

Sometimes she'd wear a black tutu, a red velvet hat, and a veil. I loved it! She always turned heads and looked drop-dead gorgeous in her vintage ensembles. We would head over to Optimo, buy a few forties with my chalked driver's license, and make our way to the F train. By the time we got to Mars, we'd march up to the velvet ropes as if we owned the place, whacked out of our minds on Old E. The doormen would take one look at Rachel and let us right in, even though we were only sixteen. Once inside, she'd flirt with men to buy us drinks.

The first night we went to Mars happened to be the Sunday before Columbus Day. We were off from school the next day, and decided that instead of renting *Blue Velvet* and watching it in my parents' basement for the eighth time, we'd head into "the city" and check out Mars. Since neither one of us had any experience in the club scene, we had no idea that Sunday was gay night. I have no idea how this started, but someone once told me that clubs turned gay on Sundays because hairdressers were off on Mondays. If this is true, I feel insulted in about 9,532 ways.

When the bouncer told us what night it was, a thrilling sensation ran up and down my spine. Rachel asked if I still wanted to go. "What the hell?" I said. "We're already here."

Once inside, whatever expectations I had of the gay community were thrown out the window. First of all, these men were in amazing shape. A lot of them were shirtless, revealing their taut, chiseled torsos. They weren't skinny and gross and awkward, like I felt. And they were Madonna fans! I was *shocked* these men were getting down to the stop-and-go-dub of Madonna's "Express Yourself" on the second floor. I thought they listened to self-hating alternative music like The Smiths in their blue, sponged bedrooms like I did.

That night marked our introduction to the club scene, and we started going every weekend. For this reason, I had a special interest in seeing what they had done to the place. Was there a sling hanging in the middle of the dance floor? Were people screwing in the corner where the cigarette machine used to be? This, and many other questions would be answered the night I convinced my friends to go a few years later. In all honesty, all it took to convince them was a pitcher of margaritas and a disposable razor.

I was having dinner with friends at Bandito's, a Mexican restaurant on Greenwich Avenue famous for using liquid crack in their margaritas. After I finished my second drink, I brazenly announced, "We're going to The Vault!" Shockingly, everyone agreed. I was with Charles, and my best friends from high school, Jessica and Heather.

As we stumbled outside to have a cigarette, Jessica and I slipped into a phone booth to see how much the cover charge was. A friendly voice told us it was $40 for men and free for women. But the men could get in free if they brought a woman with a "shaved beaver." Intrigued, we told Heather and Charles. When Heather heard she would need a shaved pussy to get in for free, she figured that was the end of it. Charles, or GC as the girls called him (for Gay Charles) raised one eyebrow and smirked. "Village Apothecary is right across the street."

Smash cut to: Interior Pizzeria Bathroom. The four of us huddled in a bathroom which measured no bigger than four by five feet. GC busted out a razor and started going to town on Jessica's crotch. Long, straggly pubes clogged the sink. Five minutes later, Jessica was finished and admiring herself in the mirror – just like Madonna in the *Sex* book! A few minutes later, GC worked his magic on Heather and we headed out the door.

Heather turned to Jessica as we snuck past the nosy owner giving us the side eye and said, "No one is going to believe this."

"That's because no one is going to find out about this," Jessica replied.

As we drove to the West Side singing along to "The Immaculate Collection," Heather peeked out the front window. "Is that the Holland Tunnel?" she asked during "Papa Don't Preach." A quick detour through Hoboken and half an hour later, we were at the Vault. Score One: Liquid Crack Margaritas. Once outside, we were greeted by a bouncer wearing a harness. He directed us to the ticket counter, where a snotty 25-year-old girl asked Charles for forty bucks.

"But they're with us and we have…we're shaved down there," Jessica replied. "Well, show it to Vinny," the woman snorted.

"What, you expect me to pull down my pants and show this guy my pussy in the middle of the lobby?"

"Yeah. If you'se wanna get in for free, that is."

Jessica sighed and exposed her privates for Vinny to inspect.

"She's good," he said, and we entered the club.

"And now you," Vinny said to Heather, who reluctantly slid her pants down as Vinny checked her out. "Wait a minute. I see hair down there."

Heather was not taking any prisoners. "Do you mean to tell me I just shaved my pussy in a pizzeria bathroom, and you're not gonna let me in?"

"No, no, it's fine. You can go in," he sheepishly responded.

"Thanks, handsome," she said as she tweaked his pencil eraser of a nipple.

Once inside, we realized the customers who frequented The Vault were straight out of the Coney Island Freak Show. A 250-pound man was on his knees in the middle of the floor licking the boots of a woman seated in a spiked medieval throne. Two other men were behind him, waiting to moisten her boots with their hungry tongues. The only other woman we saw turned out to be a transvestite dressed in a cocktail dress and a blond wig who was sitting in a sling with his/her legs in the air, fingering his/her bunghole, right next to the Ms. Pac-Man Machine.

Besides these oddities, there were a handful of thin, lecherous men milling about. It all looked like a scene out of *Schindler's List*. The only thing missing was the Nazi Uniform – wait, there it was – on that 55-year-old man smoking a Misty cigarette in the corner! Between the throne, the spikes, the costumes and wigs, I felt like I was in *Lady Chatterley's Lover*.

As we made our way through the club, I was disappointed to discover the entire five floors weren't open – but it made sense. Why open the top three floors and a roof deck for ten people? Although I would have loved to have seen "Dressed To Kill" work that roof deck. Or Hitler lounging on one of those deco couches on the third floor, which would have at least put his costume in a historically accurate context.

Since none of us had any intention on having sex, Jessica and I headed over to play Ms. Pac-Man. Thankfully, we figured out that if you stayed on the right side of the machine and didn't turn your head, you could play without seeing "Dressed to Kill" massaging his/her prostate/g-spot a few feet away. "Erotica…romance?" Not tonight.

We checked in with Charles and Heather, who confirmed we could be having the same experience without the sexual oddities in the East Village. After one quick glance at the shrimping session that was starting to heat up, we said goodbye to the Vault and headed into the night.

When all was said and done, we learned something from venturing into the seedy underbelly of NYC nightlife. I realized all the intrigue Madonna created with the release of the "Erotica"/*Sex* media blitz turned out to be nothing more than hype. But that's what you get for trying to make a fantasy a reality. For the photo shoot, Madonna stocked The Vault with models and porn stars. In reality, it was filled with skeezes and skanks. If we never went to The Vault that night, we might still have that fantasy. But we did. And as we stumbled back to Jessica's car that cool October night, we vowed never to tell anyone about what we did.

Oops.

Years later, I continued my passion for Madonna's *Sex* book by shooting a shot-for-shot parody of it called "Sex In Drag" for the 20th anniversary of its release. Here is one of the frightening images with me "dressed" as Madonna. More pictures and books available on www.sexindrag.com.*

*In the immortal words of Madonna, "I'm not the same, I have no shame."

A parody of my favorite shot of Madonna crouching on the beach like an animal.

CHAPTER 20.

MASS TRANSIT

When I first moved to Cobble Hill, Brooklyn, I thought it would be a great idea to take the F train to Coney Island one day. It was sweltering, and I figured I'd be able to lie on the beach, take a quick dip in that potato chip bag-infested ocean and maybe catch the Freak Show. I knew I'd probably run into a few unsavory characters and an illegal immigrant or two peddling empanadas, but what I didn't expect to see was the sunburned vagina of a homeless woman staring up at me as soon as I stepped on the sand.

On the way home, I saw a man eating an entire meal on the subway. This is something I have never been able to comprehend. What is wrong with these people? Are they starving? On the brink of death? Ravenous beyond words? Maybe they have low blood sugar and need to eat every hour on the hour? Although I might understand slamming down a Powerbar if one was pressed for time, the concept of consuming an entire meal on the D train is beyond me.

Then again, maybe these people don't understand the meaning of the word, ambience. I, personally enjoy sharing meals with friends and loved ones in a non-mass transit environment – on a table, if you will – or at least some sort of plate. Call me a traditionalist, but the thought of having lunch, or – Jesus Christ–dinner–on the C train repulses me because regardless of how the train looks at that moment, at some point, a homeless person took a dump on it.

In a related thought, have you ever ridden the Circle Line? They need to re-name it "The C Train of The Sea." A ride on that thing makes the Staten Island Ferry look like The Queen Elizabeth.

By the way, if you're a tourist planning on visiting NYC, do yourself a favor and take a ride on the Staten Island Ferry. Not only is it free, it's one of the best ways to view the city. In fact, whenever a friend comes to visit, I make sure to send them on it so I can get a fucking minute to myself – er – so they can go on a really great boat ride. Whatever you do, don't take the bus there. They suck.

CHAPTER 21.

GOTTA DOLLAH?

Homeless people in New York City are nameless, faceless entities. You see one one day, and the next, they're gone. But across the bridges and tunnels in Brooklyn, the homeless are a lot less transient. Like their Kings County counterparts, they tend to nest more than people in "the city."

This is a good *and* bad thing. For one, you can tell whether that homeless man who sleeps across the street in the abandoned lot is a drunk, a heroin addict, or just plain crazy. Most people don't seem to mind giving their money to a crazy person because they don't think it's going to be "wasted" on drugs or alcohol. I'm an equal-opportunity change-giver. I don't care if you're on crack – if you're homeless, you need my fifty cents more than I do. Whether it's to help you buy a sandwich or your next fix, either way, you're in much worse shape than I am. And getting off drugs is difficult. Who am I to judge?

The bad thing about seeing the same homeless people is that sooner or later, they start to feel like they can ask you for money *every time you see them*, just because you once threw a nickel at them on your way home from McHale's at 3 AM. What you didn't realize in your drunken stupor is that nickel bought you something you never imagined: your new best friend. Now, every time they see you coming down Smith Street, it's, "Hey buddy! Spare some change?"

When it gets to this stage, there are two roads to take. One: Walk around with a constant pit in your stomach, anticipating that dreaded encounter with your new best friend; or two: Start acting like you're bipolar. I find this to be the most reasonable solution because it allows you to regain control of the relationship. Trust me, your new friend will not be offended when you lash out at them because they know they just might get a dollar the next time they see you. Hey, they're homeless. Their standards are a bit lower than those uppity friends of yours who live in homes.

And just like real friends, homeless friends come in all shapes, sizes, and temperaments. Take for example, this one woman who currently haunts Pacific Street in Prospect Heights. Any time, day or night, you never know when – she can be found pushing her shopping cart as she mumbles to herself and/or points and laughs at you. Now if only I could get this woman to attend one of my one-man shows!

During the summer of 2012, my boyfriend ran into this *thing* on the way home from work. In broad daylight, she leaned against a building, lifted up her skirt, and took a dump. Instead of being mortified when she saw him approaching, she stared him down and said, "Come here baby, I've got a present for you!"

In cases like this, I must recommend the cease and desist approach. Do not engage this type of homeless person, *ever*. They will not bring you joy the way Freddie

The Heroin Addict does. At best, she will turn into that family member you have – you know, the one who calls you at midnight to discuss the intricate plot twists of a *Real Housewives of Atlanta* marathon after taking too many Xanax? Although you'd like to tell this person to hang up and never call you again, you can't, *because they're your cousin.*

One other drawback of the familial homeless person is the anxiety that develops when you stop seeing them in your neighborhood. Did they find a widescreen TV box in Park Slope? Are they in Bellevue...again...? Are they...oh God no...dead? Come to think of it, most of these questions can be hefted on your mentally ill family member, too.

I went through this terrible strain after my favorite homeless woman suddenly disappeared from her station outside of Met Food in Cobble Hill. Stella and I became fast friends when her greetings quickly progressed from "Gotta quartah?" to "Gotta dollah?" to "Give me five dollahs." For three years, I threw her a couple of bucks once or twice a week. Although I did need to pull my bipolar act on her on more than one occasion, this woman seemed to find my fits humorous. Apparently my target audience is homeless women.

Sadly, I never did see her again. Until it closed last year, I used to ride my bike over to the old Met Food to do my shopping every Monday, hoping to see her calloused face. I'd give anything to hear her mutter, "Gotta dollah?" just one more time...

CHAPTER 22.

MS. PAC-MAN FEVER

Whoever invented Super-Speed Ms. Pac-Man must have been a speed freak. I know because for a five month period back in college, I was a speed freak. And she was my best friend. It all began innocently enough, when my friend Jessica and I met up with our pot dealer, Mark, to buy some weed one night. While we were making the transaction in the back of her filthy Jetta, Mark asked if we'd like to try Ritalin, which he stole from the pharmacy he worked at. We were down. Or up, as it turned out.

One small, white pill later and there we were, in Alley Pond Park, bonding over the most painful childhood memories as we tore through a pack of Marlboro Reds in Jessica's car. Years later, when I saw Julianne Moore and Heather Graham bond while doing rails of coke in *Boogie Nights*, my mouth dropped open as they re-enacted one of our very conversations. What was with me and Paul Thomas Anderson films?

Ritalin was the best. It made you feel great, you could drink all night, and you never turned into a mess. Best of all, whenever you felt like you were coming down, you just popped half a Ritalin and went to Archeology class, which I mistakenly enrolled in after listening to The B-52's "Mesopotamia" a few too many times.

With all this extra time on our hands from avoiding tiresome activities like sleeping and eating, Jessica and I started driving into the city every night to camp out at a dive bar on 2nd Avenue and 1st Street that had a Super Speed Ms. Pac-Man machine. They also had a Super Pac-Man machine, but whoever invented that must have been on acid. It's just weird. To this day, I do not understand why Pac-Man gets all big, but never knocks into the walls of the maze?

Jessica and I would buy a few rounds of beer, get ten dollars worth of quarters and attack the joystick like there was no tomorrow. When the bar closed, we'd head over to that deli on Saint Mark's Place with the beat-up, old Ms. Pac Man right outside that wound up being featured in an episode of *Absolutely Fabulous* when Patsy and Edina visit New York. The two of us had no problem partying with the homeless people who camped outside, who bummed our half-smoked cigarettes and warm 40's since we got to play whenever we wanted to. Jessica would drop me home just before the sun rose and my father got up for work. I'd lie in bed for hours, feeling my heart beat out of my chest, plotting my next opportunity to usurp her as the Super-Speed Ms. Pac-Man Queen.

Besides having a lot of fun, we also shared a lot of therapeutic conversations. It helped that our Ritalin phase coincided with me coming out to my family. There were plenty of issues to deal with, and having a five hour therapy session while hunched over a video game was a lot more beneficial than going to that shrink my mother made me see after I told her I was gay, who told me *she* was the one who should be seeing him.

Our increasing tolerance of Ritalin came to a screeching halt when our pot dealer got fired. I can still remember that last pill we split, the one we found underneath a few 40's on the bottom of her Jetta after we heard the news. Sadly, it only gave us a little jolt, but it was enough for us to get through fifteen minutes of *Casino* before being thrown out for commenting on the film non-stop. "Do you believe what Sharon Stone is wearing? It's simply fantastic. Who's the costume designer for this picture?" "I don't know, but I think Joe Pesci is hot." "You are totally weird, you know that?" "No I'm not, he's cute...in a Napoleon sort of way." "Hey, do you know if this picture is based on a real story?" "I don't know, but I just love anything Scorsese does – look at that crane shot." "Crane shot, who do you think you are? Orson Welles?" "You can be such an asshole. You know I'm a film major. Did you even decide what you're going to major in yet?" "17th Century British Poetry." "Oh, that's gonna get you far." "Hey, do you want to go outside for a cigarette?" "Yeah, and I could use another Coke, too."

To think they give that drug to children! Doctors say it doesn't have the same effect, but if one small pill was able to turn a 150-pound man into a speed freak, I cannot begin to imagine what's going on in Little Billy's mind during penmanship. And to make matters worse, he can't even smoke!

My relationship with speed took a five-year hiatus when the media started a feeding frenzy on Ritalin as if they were dots in a Ms. Pac-Man game. Every news story seemed to center on high school students abusing the drug, and street supplies dried up. Thankfully, I found a milder substitute: cocaine. Although those constant trips to the bathroom were a little inconvenient, it provided the same jolt. It also helped that a friend of mine was a coke dealer.

Donny was the coolest drug dealer I ever met on a phone sex line. We met through an ad I found in the *Village Voice* that offered a free call to lure you into paying $3.99 a minute. This was way before smart phones and hookup apps made getting laid as easy as pressing on a glass screen five times. Since I was living at home, I had to use these opportunities to meet guys until I could afford my own phone line. In one of the first signs the universe approved of my homosexuality, the first phone number I eventually wound up with was 343-JOCK.

One Saturday afternoon, I dialed the line when my parents were at the beach and got connected with the hottest-sounding guy who claimed to be a construction worker. He had the thickest Queens accent and sounded totally straight. He told me he only had sex with one other guy and was interested in trying it again. I told him I would meet him in an hour.

Donny insisted on taking me to Breadstix, a restaurant on Queens Boulevard. He wanted to wine and dine me, and told me to wear a tie since I lost my fake ID in the back room of Disco 2000 at Limelight the week before. "Maybe we'll go out for a drink, too after," he said. *Twist my arm*, I thought. After dinner, we headed to a bar called Friends, a popular watering hole for Latin gays who called Jackson Heights their home.

After five drinks, Donny asked me if I wanted to go home with him. I thought he was insane to even think of driving back to College Point – aka the arm pit of the earth – since he was so wasted. When I asked him if he was okay to drive, he whipped out a bag of coke and said he'd be fine in ten minutes. I was in love.

After two trips to the bathroom, Donny and I became friends indeed, in the honor of the very bar we were partying in. On the way home, he pulled over at a 24-hour convenience store, and told me to buy some VCR Head Cleaner. After I got back in the car, I handed him the small brown bottle I assumed was going to fix his problematic VCR. Instead, he popped open the bottle, shoved it up his nose, huffed away and went down on me right inside the parking lot.

If VCR Head Cleaner made someone give head like this, it would be my duty to make sure all the VCR's in the world would remain in need of its services for the rest of my life. Donny informed me it wasn't really VCR Head Cleaner, but poppers, aka amyl nitrate, which a lot of gay men use to heighten sexual excitement. It seemed that one man Donny slept with had taught him a lot.

After a few lines on his black enamel coffee table, Donny said he could get me coke whenever I wanted. So not only was he a straight-acting construction worker who sucks dick like there's no tomorrow, but he also deals drugs? I was in love. And who was I to judge him for having bad taste in furniture or for living in a neighborhood that was created after the town dump was covered with landfill?

Over the course of the next few years, Donny and I became close friends. The sex fell to the wayside, as we both found boyfriends who thankfully hit it off. My boyfriend, Paul and I used to head over to his apartment on Saturday nights, have a few drinks and then head over to one of the gay bars on Roosevelt Avenue in Jackson Heights.

My re-introduction to the world of speed happened during one of our Saturday night get-togethers. As we were having one of Donny's famous Vodka and Minute Maid fruit punch cocktails he swore were better than Jesus' wine, I spied a small brown vial on the coffee table, right at the foot of his plastic statue of David. I opened the vial, took out a key and did a quick bump.

Before Donny could even jump up off his black linoleum floor and rip the vial out of my hand, it hit me. "What the fuck are you doing? That's crystal meth!" he screamed.

"Never heard of it," I snapped. Since this was years before the meth epidemic, I figured it was just a stronger version of cocaine. Little did I know.

"One bump and you'll be up all night long," he said.

"Yeah, right. I only did the smallest k-k-k-k-key," I stuttered. My heart started pounding. The plastic statue of David stared up at me mockingly. The paranoia had set in. I was starting to feel like that time I accidentally smoked crack in Central Park!

Thirty minutes later, we were at Krash, a nightclub on Steinway Street which played Salsa and Meringue at the most ear-deafening levels while busboys partied in their International Male Exclusives. As I stepped into the nightclub, I looked over to see…a Ms. Pac-Man Machine! I ran straight over and embraced my long-lost friend. They say God works in coincidences – serendipity, if you will – and if that's the case, then I know God was with me on all of those speedy nights, saying hello to me through a yellow woman with a red bow in her hair and an insatiable appetite.

Paul handed me a quarter and I started playing. I should have known something was wrong when my entire body broke into a sweat and I started shaking. Sweat poured down the screen, but I couldn't stop playing! And for some reason, this Super-Speed Ms. Pac-Man just wasn't fast enough!!! Maybe it had something to do with the drugs, or the fact that the joystick kept slipping out of my hands, but after eleven terrible games, I had yet to reach the act where Ms. Pac Man gives birth. It was time for a drink. I headed to the bar and slammed down a vodka cranberry.

For some reason, the music was great!!! I headed to the floor and danced for two hours straight. I kept wondering why my friends wanted to keep taking breaks for things like drinks and bathroom breaks. I had so much energy!

At 4 AM, Donny dragged me off of the dance floor and made me have some water. He announced, "That's it. Club's closin'. We're getting the fuck outta here." I sidled up to Paul, who was now three sheets to the wind, and downed a bottle of Poland Spring on the way back to the car. Since he was drunk and I had lost the ability to focus hours ago, we decided to "sleep" at Donny's. Unfortunately, his spare bedroom was only accessible through a spiral staircase in the middle of his living room.

After moving the ceramic Mary on a Half Shell and Jesus that he kept at the foot of the stairs, I was able to steer Paul up the stairs and into bed. An hour later, I was still lying in bed, wide-awake, just like the old days. At 6 AM, I headed downstairs to hang out with David, Mary and Jesus to watch some TV. My head was aching, my body was sore, and my mind would not stop racing.

At that point, I realized there is nothing good on television at 6 AM. What ever happened to *The 700 Club* or *Davie & Goliath*? After flipping through thousands of channels, there was no choice but to put on one of Donny's porn videos. After the video started playing (God, his VCR heads were clean) I realized there was no way I would be able to do anything remotely sexual with Mary and Jesus just a stone's throw away.

Around 7 AM, I realized his kitchen needed cleaning. I don't know why anyone would get black *everything* in their kitchen. Every single water stain shows! Thank God his latest Latin boyfriend was a neat freak, because there was plenty of Fantastico! to get that place sparkling clean by the time everybody rose to start their day. The smell of bacon and eggs frying did nothing to settle my nerves, and since the grease stains were going to be a bitch to clean up, I got out of dodge.

Paul and I thanked our hosts and headed back to Brooklyn. It was now 2 PM and I still hadn't slept. But I did have a vague sense of needing nourishment, so I ate some veggie nuggets. After two bites, I had to lay down. Fourteen hours later, I woke up, my bed sheets covered in sweat. I stumbled out of bed and vowed to never touch speed again.

And I haven't. Since then, I've watched people who are on coke or speed and thought, "Did I rock back and forth while clenching my jaw? Did I light a new cigarette with the one I was just finishing? Did I speak for twenty minutes straight without letting anyone else interject?" In short, was I a wreck? The answer: Yes. But that's what people in their twenties do. I was young and adventurous, trying drugs for rebellion and discovery. But once I discovered what they did to my mind, body and soul, I stopped. Eventually, most of my friends did, too. The ones who didn't are still rebelling against things they don't want to discover.

Even though I never became addicted to drugs, I did get addicted to something else: working out. Exercising fulfills many needs in me, and at the same time, releases endorphins that make me feel wonderful, clear and focused. And thanks to the realization that 35-year olds will buy anything nostalgic, I was able to buy a plug–and-play Ms. Pac-Man on Amazon, which I attack in my living room after thirty-minute runs. And best of all, my strawberry/banana smoothie tastes so much better than that stale forty...

CHAPTER 23.

COFFEE TALK

My boyfriend, Paul is a coffee freak. Mind you, calling someone you've been with for twenty-one years a "boyfriend" is just plain ridiculous. But since he's not a fan of the expression, "gay male life partner," let's just stick with boyfriend. But I digress. Within seconds of rising, the machine is on, and in minutes, there is a giant mug poured and ready to be consumed. I, on the other hand, cannot even look at the stuff. Just one sip will make me nervous and jittery, and an entire cup will ensure a nervous breakdown...after I finish scrubbing the bathroom.

The worst part about his coffee habit is that I roll out of bed around 9:00 like a zombie and need two full hours to rise to a normal state of consciousness. Paul, who is up at the crack of dawn, is already driving his mind at 65MPH when I arise, thanks to all the caffeine sparking his synapses. As I stumble into the living room, trying to figure out what world I am in, he will blurt out random statements that completely confound me.

At first, I felt the need to respond to them all, but eventually realized I didn't have to because another bizarre statement was just fifteen seconds away. If I did answer, I'd wind up having a heated discussion on the plight of the farmer or the monogamous nature of the meerkat; two things I could care less about.

So the next time he announces real estate prices have reached a new high in Brooklyn, I'll just rub the sleep out of my eyes and brace myself for the monologue on local produce that is sure to follow.

CHAPTER 24.

TEN, NINE, FLARB

Never host a New Year's Eve Party on mushrooms. The hallucinogenic properties of the fungi make you completely unaware of the concept of time, and before you know it, some Type-A woman will run up and say, "Where's the champagne and noisemakers? It'll be 1998 in ten seconds!" After you stare at her for an inordinate amount of time trying to remember what seconds are, you will burst out laughing in her face. "Happy New Year!" she'll reply, and you'll think, "Her eyebrows look funny."

CHAPTER 25.

SHOWGIRLS

A few years after we graduated from Hunter College, my friend, Charles moved to Fort Lauderdale to be closer to his family, who had relocated there while he was in school. I made it my business to visit him as often as I could, since we remained good friends even after he moved away. Fort Lauderdale is a great place to visit if you're gay, since just about every shopping mall has a leather bar right next to an Olive Garden.

When he first left NYC, Charles had to move in with his parents because he couldn't afford a place of his own. His mother, Kara, was a tough Irish woman who chain-smoked Marlboros in between stints of boiling meat for breakfast, lunch and dinner. I loved her, since she did not mince words and you always knew just where you stood with her.

Since I was just out of college and practically broke, I had to stay at his parent's house and sleep on their busted pull out couch the first time I visited. Each morning, I'd wake up with a backache. Thankfully, Kara was also generous with her pills, and I'd be flying high on Percoset before we hit the beach.

The week I was visiting, a plane crashed in the Everglades, and Kara was obsessed with the story. All week long, she sat in the kitchen watching CNN while updating everyone when they passed by. "They found another body," she'd say as she stubbed out a cigarette in her overburdened ashtray. "That'll probably be the last one, what with the alligators and all. I'm sure it's just gonna be body parts from here on in." As if for emphasis, she'd chuck a roast beef into a pot of boiling water.

Charles always made sure to stay on her good side because he needed to borrow her car if we wanted to go out at night. Unbeknownst to her, he had been taking me to gay bars and strip clubs all week long. The concept of a gay strip club was novel to me, since we didn't have any in New York. The closest thing we had was a hustler bar called Stella's, where illegal immigrants would rub their lycra-sheethed members against your hand for ten dollars. It was either that, or Chippendales, where gay men were only welcome on stage. But in Fort Lauderdale, there was an actual strip club *for* gay men *featuring* gay men!

When you first entered the club, there was a large, rectangular bar and a few pool tables. Looking around, you'd think you were in any old watering hole. But in the corner of the room was a Plexiglas door that led to the stripper room. To the left of that was a small room with two benches and a red light dangling from the ceiling. I have no idea what the purpose of that room was, but I was soon to find out one of its uses.

The club was a blast. The dancers were hilarious, and had no shame in stripping to a Donna Summer or Kylie Minogue song. The clientele varied between young guys out for a hoot, lecherous old men, and a truck driver or two taking a break after a long haul. After a few lap dances from men with names like "Precious," "Luscious" and "Sledgehammer," Charles and I headed to that little red room to have a cigarette. As fate would have it, Madonna's "Erotica" came blasting over the stereo and I started giving him a lap dance.

I gyrated on his lap as if I were Elizabeth Berkeley in "Showgirls." That's when I noticed a truck driver seated directly across from us. I laughed and nervously got off Charles' lap. The trucker lit a cigarette, looked at me and said, "Don't stop." Then he reached into his jeans and pulled out a twenty-dollar bill. I sat back down to consider my new career as an erotic dancer. Realizing the opportunity ahead of us, Charles got up, grabbed the bill and said, "Now where's one for him?" The trucker laughed, reached into his pocket and gave him another twenty. Charles snatched it up. By now "Erotica" had ended and I came to the sad realization I would have to give him a lap dance to the tune of Pebbles' "Mercedes Boy." Would the degradation ever cease?

Knowing the forty bucks would buy us a few more rounds and maybe another lap dance from Luscious, I straddled Charles and continued my impersonation of Nomi Malone. This time, I recreated the scene when she's getting fucked by Kyle MacLachlan in the pool. I threw my body to the ground and gyrated like I was being electrocuted. When the song came to an end, the trucker thanked us and headed into the night.

As soon as he left, we headed to the bar and did a few shots. And then a few more. When the bar closed a few hours later, neither of us were in any condition to drive. Thankfully, the bartender called us a cab and we headed back home.

Early the next morning, all hell broke loose. The second she woke up, Kara noticed her car was missing. While I was passed out on the sofa bed, I heard her scream, "Charles! Where the hell is my car? Get out of bed and tell me where it is now!" Two seconds later, Charles was up and trying to placate her. "Mother, I lost the keys in the club last night. The car is parked in the middle of Ekard's Shopping Center. There's nothing to worry about." "Don't you show me sass like that. I'll slap your face!" she screamed. "Mother," Charles snapped, "I think you're being dramatic and –" THWACK! She had indeed slapped his face. "Now go get my car."

Her Lincoln was right where we left it in the middle of the strip mall parking lot. By the time we got home, Kara must have forgotten the whole thing because her only comment was, "They found another arm in the Everglades." Somehow, Charles was able to convince her to let him borrow her car again that night so we could see a porn star who was performing at the gay bar next to Petland Discounts. God, I just love Fort Lauderdale.

CHAPTER 26.

GOD IS A DJ

An angel descended from the heavens and appeared before me. Weaving her hands to and fro, she lured me closer and closer as she cast her magical spell. Twirling fingers beckoned me through smoke and swirling lights. Her eyes penetrated the darkness – and my soul. I was in a feverish trance and no longer knew where I ended and she began.

Man was I high.

"Watch over the fried piker. The fuzzy hitch is lazy," I heard from out of nowhere. "Huh?" I asked the darkness. Someone pulled me close. "I said, watch out for the Pied Piper. That fucking bitch is crazy." I stared at this mysterious figure, trying to sort out who and what it is. "Come on, we're taking a break, " it said. It led me off the dance floor, shoved a bottle of water in my hand and said, "Drink this. Now." I followed its orders and realized I was thirsty beyond belief. What time was it? How long was I dancing for? Was it day or night?

The water cooled me down, and I floated back down to reality. "Greg, are you alright?" I turned to the voice and began to realize it was coming from the mouth of my friend, Kevin. Oh, so that's who this was.

The bastard! For the first time in my history of taking ecstasy, it had worked. And now he was trying to ruin it by making me drink water? What kind of friend was he? I would kill him if I didn't love him so much.

"That girl's a whack job. I call her Crackzilla because she's always cracked out of her mind. She gets her thrills by fucking with people when they're high." And here I thought an angel had come to guide me through the night.

As my eyes came back into focus, I realized where I was – in the lounge of Body & Soul. There was no mistaking this place, as it was decorated in that factory break room décor which always made one feel like luxuriating: wooden couches covered in the same industrial-grade carpeting as the floor, metal folding chairs and whatever paint they found in the bargain bin at Home Depot slapped on the walls. But nobody went to Body & Soul for the glamour. They went there to get down. So why spend a fortune turning it into something out of "Wallpaper" magazine if everyone was just going to show up in sweat pants?

It was my kind of club. There was no attitude, people came to dance, and the music was amazing. You weren't going to get any "Now That's What I Call Dance!" crap here – just pure, soulful house and disco classics. On its best nights, going to Body & Soul was like attending a block party in Bed Stuy – minus the Merry Go Round. I take that back. If the drugs were good, you *were* on a Merry Go Round. Or one of those throw-up rides. It just depended on how good the shit was.

In my experience, no ecstasy trip was the same. Sometimes I'd drop a hit only to turn fetal in the corner as the rest of my friends found God on the dance floor. Other times, it turned out to be pure speed, and I'd wind up chomping on gum and smoking a pack of cigarettes, feverishly talking to strangers between drags. "And then in fifth grade…" I'd go on. But inevitably, it always came back to my third grade teacher, Mrs. Kuznitz. That aptly-named beast tortured me for an entire year because I didn't hold my pencil "right." Every day I was singled out because I didn't hold the pencil *like everyone else.* Well guess, what, Mrs. Cunt-tits? I still hold my pencil wrong. Unlike David Wentworth, who held his pencil right and is currently in jail. As you can see, sometimes I'd go down a very dark spiral. But this time, I'd gotten the real deal. "Wow, this stuff is great," I told Kevin as I slammed down another bottle of water. "You're right. This is nothing like that time on Fire Island." Jeez, why did he have to bring that up? This guy was turning out to be a real buzz kill.

A few years back, the two of us rented a house in Cherry Grove for a week one August. For some odd reason, we both had jobs that year and were able to afford an oceanfront house instead of that musty, old shack by the bay we usually rented. While laying on the beach one afternoon, Kevin told me his friend Kyle was coming to visit that night, along with his boyfriend, Sam, and their ecstasy dealer, Joy.

Now maybe it's the way I was raised, but I always bring something when I go to someone's house. Whether it's a bottle of wine or a magnum of wine, I never show up empty-handed. Especially if I'm bringing friends. But not Kyle. When he marched through our door later that day, he handed me a half-eaten bag of Salt & Vinegar potato chips and said, "Thanks for having us. We weren't planning on opening them, but that ferry ride was soooooo long." Hmmm. The last time I checked, it was twenty minutes long.

But these people looked like they traveled to all ends of the earth, instead of on the Long Island Railroad and the ferry like the rest of us. Kyle had bags under his eyes and smelled like Camembert cheese. Kevin said it was because he was "earthy," but after spending a few days with him, I think "depraved" was a much better description. His boyfriend Sam was an Aborigine hairdresser who was currently sporting a zebra Mohawk and matching sarong. Joy, as she was so un-aptly named, was a Filipino mother of two who looked like the Zuni Fetish doll from "Trilogy of Terror." She had a mouth full of jagged, toasted pignoli nut teeth and wore what appeared to be a large woven basket of hair atop her head. To make her even more endearing, every once in a while she'd let out a cackle that made me want to throw her in the oven.

I never would have let these degenerates into our home, but since they had drugs, Kevin and the rest of our housemates welcomed them with open arms. Another flag went up when Kyle started making cocktails for everyone with the liquor I schlepped on the island. Filling six pint glasses with gin and topping them off with a twist of lime, he announced, "This drink is gonna be just like heaven. I am soooooo looking forward to a relaxing week."

Come again?

Not one to let things slide, I pulled Kevin aside and asked him what was going on. "Oh, it must have been a slip. He's gotta manage the restaurant tomorrow night. They're leaving in the morning." Or a few mornings after that, as it turned out.

"We have more gin, right?" Kyle asked as he topped off his drink with the last of the Bombay ten minutes later. Four hours later, they had polished off the rum and were working through the vodka. "Anyone want a drink?" Kyle asked, always the host. I guess he thought no one would remember he'd been using all of our liquor if he served them until they passed out. Now I've never been one to mask the way I feel about people, and Kyle must have caught on, as most bottom feeders do. Although they seem to be clueless, they know just what they're doing. So, as he handed me a vodka cranberry with a fucking umbrella, he told me he planned on going to the liquor store in the morning. "I'd go tonight, but that trip just *wiped me out.*"

For someone who was *wiped out*, he certainly had a lot of energy. While Kevin and I cooked dinner, he insisted on scanning the beach for table garnish. "A proper dinner is never complete without table garnish," he announced as he threw a pinecone on my plate.

Dinner consisted of four magnums of Pinot Grigio and a fork-full of salmon, as he and his friends were on Atkins (read = alcoholics.) After their "meal" came to an end around the time the rest of us started our salads, Joy announced she was handing out treats to anyone who wanted them. Hmm, so maybe these people weren't dirt bags after all. If a hit of ecstasy was twenty-five dollars, then four of them would make a very nice hostess gift. In that case, I could put up with a depleted liquor cabinet and these lowlifes. "That'll be twenty five dollars," she said as she slipped the pill in my hand.

As usual, all the ecstasy did was make me sit in the corner, rocking back and forth with my hands around my knees. But not the rest of the house. Everyone was rocking out to the "Body & Soul Vol. 3? compilation I slipped into the CD player. At two AM, I headed to the deck as I waited for the drugs to kick in. At one point, Joy saw me cowering on the chaise lounge and came over to comfort me. "You just need to get in there and let it do its thing. You'll be feeling great in no time." Two hours later, I was still on that chaise lounge, watching Kyle as he polished off the last of the vodka with a round of kamikaze shots.

Before he finished our entire supply, I decided to make a break for the kitchen to hide the tequila, which he hadn't spied yet. There was no way I was going to let this skeeze finish off all our booze only to sneak away on the ten o'clock ferry! I found the tequila and snuck off to bed with two bottles weighing down my cargo pants. As I said goodnight to my friends, I noticed everyone was in the process of taking another hit. "That'll be twenty five dollars," Joy said brightly.

I crawled down to the lower level to try and fall asleep. Since the ecstasy never hit me, I figured I'd be out in no time. What I didn't expect was their dance party to rock on until eleven in the morning. At one point, I honestly thought they led a circus elephant into the house and were having it do parlor tricks. The ceiling creaked and bellowed as dust and wood shavings floated around my sleepless body.

At ten AM, I marched upstairs to find out what was going on. I blinked twice and saw Kyle in the middle of a tribal dance in the living room, jumping up and down to "I Ran So Far Away." I wish I had run away. Visions of *The Exorcist* popped into my mind as I watched his arms flailing about his head, which was rolling back and forth. If this is what a good ecstasy trip was like, I'm glad I never had one. Over on the couch, Sam and Joy were having cocktails. Now what kind of cocktail could they possibly have concocted? I sauntered over to the kitchen, where I found a bottle of Triple Sec and three limes laying on the counter.

"Want a margarita?" Kyle asked as he took a break from his epileptic fit to play hostess once again. "It's eleven AM," I told him. "Is it?" he announced as he threw a splash of Triple Sec and squeezed a lime into a glass. "I had no idea." He took a sip from his "drink" and said, "Mmm. You sure?" I got acid reflux just looking at that thing and went back to bed.

Five hours later, I awoke to find the entire house empty. I headed to the deck, where I saw Kyle and Sam playing pro kidima on the beach. I looked in the living room and saw that 9,000 seashells were converted into ashtrays and every single surface was covered with half-filled glasses. Still a little tweaked from the night before, I decide to clean the house.

Thankfully, Kevin and the rest of the house passed out. They slept the whole day, leaving me in peace after I emptied the dishwasher for the fifth time. I headed to the beach to take a nap as they roused from their slumber just as the sun started to set. I laid my blanket down and listened as the waves lulled me to sleep...

"Hey, you find a ring?" some*thing* shrieked at me as I started to drift off.

"What?" I said.

"A ring. I was out here early this morning and I lost my ring." I looked up to see a gigantic woman with bright red hair towering over me. "I'm so f'in pissed I lost it," she said as she got down on her hands and knees and started sifting through the sand. "I loved that ring. My best friend gave it to me."

"Well, what makes you think you lost it here?" I asked.

"Well, I was partying with two guys on the beach here this morning. Things got real hot and heavy and my ring must have slipped off while we were having sex."

Insert record scratch.

So this woman had sex with Kyle and Sam? Jesus. If a good ecstasy trip meant having sex with this thing, I'd much rather be whimpering in the corner obsessing over Mrs. Kuznitz. "Well, let me know if you find it. I'm staying at the Ice Palace," she announced as she stampeded down the beach.

"Come on, let's get back on the dance floor," Kevin said, snapping his fingers to bring me back to reality at Body & Soul.

"Wow. How long was I zonked out for?"

"Honey, you've been zonked the whole night, but that's not gonna stop us from tearing up that dance floor. Come on, they're playing Shalamar!"

CHAPTER 27.

HOUSEWARES

Never have a three-way with someone you meet through the personal ads of a gay nightlife magazine. The one time my boyfriend and I tried it, we slept with a seemingly nice guy who wound up calling a week later to ask if he could bake Special K in our oven. Apparently, the gas in his apartment had been turned off and he needed a little cat tranquilizer to take the edge off.

Like a dumbass, I told him to come over. He baked his Special K in a pyrex dish my grandmother gave me and was on his way in an hour. Thankfully, I never saw him again. Although, to this day, I think of him whenever I make shrimp scampi.

CHAPTER 28.

PITTER PATTER

"That reminds me of the time my boyfriend made me drink a gallon of gin to bring on an abortion," I heard as I served the ginger shrimp dumplings. "Well, did it work?" I asked as all my dinner guest's mouths fell open. "How the hell should I know? It turns out I wasn't pregnant. But at least he showed me a good time." Typical Christine, who has made a career out of dropping statements like this into conversation whenever she feels left out. It's her way of reminding people she's there...as if anyone could forget the 60 year old woman wearing a red wig and an orange sweater dress.

From the first day we worked together at Radio Mexico, I "got her." While all the other waiters hated her because she'd yell at them when they tried to eat leftover wings out of the bus bin, I welcomed her bluntness. She was realer than real, and most people just don't know how to deal with that. Snobs commented on her Staten Island accent, but I found it endearing. My sisters commented on the fact that she always wore a different wig, but I found her ever-changing identity refreshing. People recoiled as she referenced childhood molestations over cocktails, but I found her openness daring. She forced you to realize life wasn't perfect – but that was no reason to start feeling sorry for yourself or blame other people for your problems. She was the penultimate self-help guru, and always knew the right thing to say. Whenever I was lost, she shined a light at the end of the tunnel, bringing me through to the other side.

We quickly bonded over a forty bag of coke the first night we worked together. After the restaurant closed, she invited me to her favorite bar, The Kastro, on East 5th street for a drink. Within minutes of being there, I knew I was home. Richard, the bartender, made me one of his world-famous margaritas, and we waited, along with the rest of the bar, for the arrival of Valeria, the coke dealer.

There was no mistaking her when she finally stepped through the door. She was a stone-faced Puerto Rican in her early 40's who was dressed in a style I can only describe as "Mother of The Bride." She wore a purple floor-length gown covered in rhinestones with matching pumps and earrings. Why someone who dealt drugs for a living would choose to be so flashy was beyond me. All anyone needed to do was tell the police to look for the brassy-haired Puerto Rican in the sequin gown if they wanted to turn her in. But that was Valeria's M.O. I would comment on whatever she was wearing – "Valeria, I just love that gold and black pant suit" – buy a forty bag of coke, and be on my way.

Christine would relay tragic stories of her upbringing as we took turns buying rounds of margaritas. She seemed to know everyone at the Kastro, and I loved meeting these bizarre creatures of the night – some of whom changed genders depending on the weather. Mark, a painter, would sometimes show up in drag, as his alter ego, Julie. As opposed to regular drag queens, who *live* for the spotlight, Julie preferred to sit in an unlit corner and flirt with straight men. I guess she figured if it was dark enough, they might not realize this 6'3? woman with an Adam's apple was really a man.

Our Sunday night trips soon became Sunday and Wednesday night trips. When I started catching later trains back to Bellerose, Christine told me she sometimes went to an after-hours club named Brownie's. Two hours later, I found myself stumbling there at 4:30AM.

When we got to the club, Christine told me to stay behind her as she knocked on the door. Ten seconds later, a very good-looking man opened up. It was Dominic, the bouncer. Christine said hello and introduced me. "And this is my friend Greg," she said. "He's good people." "Cool, Greg, nice to meet you. I'm Dominic," he said as he extended his hand. God, these after hours people were classy. "Quick, get in," he said as we scooted down the steps into the dungeon that was Brownie's.

Once inside, my eyes adjusted to the darkness and I realized I was surrounded by dirty stay-outs drinking canned beer and cocktails out of plastic cups. Although everyone was high, there was only a low hum of conversation. These after hours people really did have class! Christine and I stumbled over to the bar and lit a cigarette. "What the fuck is going on?" I asked her. "Excuse me, young man, what did you just say?" I heard from behind me. "Oops – I forgot to tell you the rules," Christine said.

I turned around to see a portly 55 year-old black man in a cowboy hat. "Young man, I will have you know that cursing is not allowed in this establishment." I turned to Christine, "Who the hell is this clown?" I whispered. "He's

Brownie," she told me. "And he takes these rules seriously." "I will not have anyone using swear words, and I take it you will follow these rules, or do I have to ask you to leave?" he continued. He was serious. "Uh, no, I had no idea – but now that I do – you won't have any trouble with me." He smiled. "That's what I thought. Miss Christine doesn't hang around trash," he said, and kissed her on the cheek. She blushed. "Oh, Brownie, stop."

It dawned on me that Christine and Brownie were lovers. If I wasn't so coked up, my heart would have stopped right there. "See you later, Brownie," Christine said, as she ushered me over to the pool table. "I just love that rule of his," Christine said. "Since people can get so messed up when they party, the fact that you know there's a small rule you need to adhere to keeps your subconscious mind aware that you need to stay under control. It's a great way to keep people in line without having to be forceful, don't you think?" "Uh...what?" I asked. She had lost me at "adhere." But in hindsight, her theory made a lot of sense. As I sat around, snorting coke off a pool table, I knew there was something I was forbidden to do, and it kept me in check.

That was the best thing about Brownie's – since it was an illegal club, there was no reason to take that long, unnecessary trip to the bathroom – all one needed to do was whip out your drugs in the middle of the bar. I soon learned this wasn't the best tactic, as lowlifes would run over acting like your best friend. I had a lot to learn about all these after-hours clubs. While I tried to sort out the do's and don'ts, I heard someone banging on the front door.

Everyone froze and looked at Dominic. A hush came over the room as he went to investigate. He came back and told everyone to head to the other side of the room in silence. Like cattle, we shuffled over to the side of the club, awaiting more instructions against a dank wall. Since I was totally out of my mind, I was convinced there were mobsters with machine guns on the other side of that door, trying to get in so they could mow us down. In reality, it was probably just the cops responding to a noise complaint. I whispered to Christine, "Has this ever happened before?" "No," she said. "Not in all the years I've come here." So the gangsters had chosen the night I came to gun people down! Seconds felt like minutes felt like hours! And still no word from Dominic!

When the thuds died down a few minutes later, he told us we couldn't leave for at least an hour. Great. So now I was trapped in a literal dungeon at 6 in the morning with no hope of getting out. "Baby, it's gonna be okay. This reminds me of the time my foster father locked me in the basement for two days when I lived in Michigan." "What happened? How did you get out?" I asked. "Well, I finally crawled out the window above the washing machine and went to my case worker and told her what happened. She placed me in a new home and that guy didn't molest me like the first one, so it all worked out fine. You see, there's always a window open for you, waiting for you to find it, even in the darkest of places."

I was in no mood for her New Age nonsense. "So where's that window now?" I asked. "How the hell should I know? This place is a rat trap. If there was a fire, we'd all be dead." Thankfully, that window did present itself two minutes later, when Brownie told Christine he was "getting out of dodge" and heading back to Brooklyn.

Once at the door, Dominic checked to make sure East 9th Street was clear. He opened it up to admit us into the blazing sunlight. Normally, I would have been completely depressed to greet the day in this condition, but after what I had been through, I was thrilled.

Two hours later, as I was lying in bed trying to fall asleep, I ran parts of the night through my head. What kept coming back to me was Christine's comment about how she was happy about getting a new foster father after being molested. It suddenly hit me and I realized why I had no problem listening to this woman's agonizing stories. Although they were horrifying, she had a way of looking at them that made me laugh. Comedy was her way of dealing with the tragedies in her life; something I related to ever since that fat bitch who lived above Bellini's Pizzeria called me "Gaygory" when I was five. But even though Christine and I were able to find humor in the abuses she experienced as a child, my friends didn't. In fact, they were often traumatized whenever she shared one of her tales.

Years later, after the Kastro and Brownie's had come to pass like so many gems of NYC, I invited Christine over for a New Year's Eve dinner party. During dessert, she shared a story about how she spent her weekends as a child on Staten Island. "Every Friday night, I sat at the dining room table with my mother and helped her melt paraffin wax so she could fill in the missing teeth in her mouth before she went to the bar. A few hours later, she would stumble back home with a strange man, wake me up and said, 'This is your *real* father.' Then she'd go have sex with him on the pullout couch."

While I howled with laughter, the fondue forks fell out of my dinner guests' hands. "So how did you feel about that?" I asked. Without missing a beat, she replied, "How the hell should I know? But I sure did love making them fake teeth. Every night was like Halloween."

CHAPTER 29.

CHECK, PLEASE

A friend of mine who lives on Fire Island decided to deal with his life-long drinking problem by joining A.A a few years ago. Part of me was upset because we would (probably?) never share another evening like the time he unzipped his pants, took his penis out and placed it in the glass of a woman who was complaining about not having enough olives in her martini. With his dick in her drink, he looked down and said, "Many people find this garnish a lot tastier," and cracked up laughing, along with the rest of the bar.

For someone who had hit rock bottom time and again, I wondered what finally made him sober up. When I asked, he relayed the following story: One night, after drinking at a bar in Fire Island Pines, he went back to his apartment in Cherry Grove through the Meat Rack, an area between the two towns where men cruise for sex. As he made his way through the woods, he came across a strapping black man. He sidled up next to him and asked, "So how's it going tonight, big guy?" When the man ignored him, he snapped, "So it's going to be like that, huh?" and stormed off. As he brushed past this hunk, he realized he was talking to a plastic bag that had blown into a tree. He hasn't had a drink since.

CHAPTER 30.

SO THIS IS WHY THEY HATE AMERICANS

"Jessica, they would have eaten you alive," John said as he drunkenly stumbled through our darkened flat at 6AM. "What are you talking about?" I asked as he tried to light the wrong end of a cigarette. "That after hours club. They would have eaten you alive," he repeated. "Will you put that thing out!? You're inhaling burnt filter," I told him. "Oh," he said, as he threw the cigarette into a beer can.

After lighting the right end of a new cigarette, John went on to tell us about the after hours club he stumbled upon after we left him in a pub six hours ago. "It was absolute chaos. Hoodlums, thugs, and a host of London's most dangerous and depraved night owls for as far as the eye could see." "Can we go now?" Jessica said. "Do you think they're still open?" "No, they closed, but you wouldn't last one minute there," John said as he ashed on the duvet cover. "They'll eat you *alive*."

With an introduction like that, did he really expect us *not* to go? We were from New York, and had been going to clubs since high school. And besides, how rough could an after hours club be if they let a theatre queen like John in? What did he do – threaten to burn his bootleg VHS copy of "Carrie: The Musical" to get in? At 6'2? and 140 pounds, he wasn't exactly menacing. In fact, the only time I ever saw him get mad was when someone sang "And I Am Telling You I'm Not Going" at karaoke just before he planned to.

Jessica and I knew whatever this club had in store, we could handle it. We ushered John into his bedroom and decided to let him sleep the day away while we toured London – then we'd wake him up in time to take us to the club. Amazingly, he slept just three hours and was ready to tour the town by the time we finished breakfast. He must have still been drunk because he lagged behind us all day long and needed to stop for drinks, food, and cigarettes every fifty feet.

Why I continued to vacation with this person for the next ten years is beyond me. In Rio, when we drove past the hotel we had been staying at for four nights, he turned to the taxi driver and said, "Is this Sao Paulo?" In Amsterdam, he whipped out a giant map in the Red Light District at 3 AM in the middle of the street. "Put that thing away," I told him. "You're like a walking target." "What's the big deal?" he said. "We're tourists. They expect this of us!"

Maybe so, but who would choose to be labeled a tourist if they could avoid doing so? I always made an effort to study the place I was visiting, and even went so far as to learn a few phrases in the native tongue. But not John. He was more than content pointing to his cigarette in Brazil and asking the waiter, "Una ashtray por favor." Or stopping random people on the street to ask where he could buy hash. While it might be legal to buy drugs in Amsterdam, did he really think that 75 year old grandmother knew where the best space cakes were sold?

So it came as no surprise to Jessica and I when we wound up making friends with everyone at this "depraved" after hours spot later that night. Within minutes, I befriended the door person and got us all in. By four-thirty, Jessica made friends with Antonio, an adorable Italian she started making out with in the middle of the lounge. By six o'clock, we were dancing on the coffee tables. We knew it was probably time to leave when we heard the door person tell the bartender, "Those people from New York won't leave." Thankfully, we decided to take the party back to our flat before they threw us out. "John, are you retarded? What makes you think they would have eaten me alive?" Jessica asked as she finally turned in. "I guess I underestimated you," he said as he tried to light the wrong end of another cigarette.

Five hours later, we were on a plane for Amsterdam. John was thrilled, because he knew he could smoke hash in the streets without having to worry about getting arrested, like he was apt to do in New York. I stopped smoking pot after college, since it only made me paranoid, but since we were in Amsterdam, I took John's advice and decided to try one of their famous space cakes.

It probably wasn't the best idea to eat the whole thing and then board a small boat for a nighttime tour of the canals. As the hash hit me, I realized I would have to sit across from a 45 year-old woman from Arkansas who was just *thrilled* to be in Europe. Before I knew it, I lost the ability to speak, and my eyes lost focus. Paranoia set in – the kind I would only imagine people with multiple personality disorder get – and I was stuck on a boat that measured four feet by eight feet with a bunch of strangers…and John.

The paranoia really kicked in when the motor on the boat stopped working and we glided towards one of the walls of the canal. "Ah…ooh…sorry…can you reach your hand out to brace the boat before it hits the –" Bam! The boat crashed into the wall, and the guide turned angrily towards me. "Did you not hear me when I asked you to grab hold of the wall?" he asked. I burst out laughing. I was completely high and was convinced this whole thing was staged. "Yeah – I just spent thirty bucks to get on a boat that crashes into a wall and *you're* mad at *me*? I've never been on a boat before – I'm no deck hand," I said as I laughed at him.

Everyone on the boat stopped to look at me. Worry plagued each face. "Greg, this is serious," John told me. I scoffed at him. "John, there is no way this is serious. What morons would run a tour company and use shitty boats that crash into the walls of the canal!?! What do you take me for? This is a hoax." "Sir, I assure you, this is no joke. Does anyone on board happen to know how to re-start a motor?" the tour guide asked. I could take no more. "Yeah, right! Not only does the motor break down, but the person who's running the boat doesn't even know how to re-start it? Are you people dumb? This person is pulling a prank! Where's the hidden camera?" I asked. When John got up to re-start the motor, I realized it wasn't a joke.

That half-hour boat ride wound up lasting two hours, but in my mind, it felt like three and a half weeks. The boat kept breaking down, and I had to pee really bad. When we finally got back on land, John was ready to hit the bars, but I couldn't even stand. I was still out of my mind, and lasted one beer before getting thrown out for walking into a wall.

John was kind enough to walk me home before heading back out for the night. I crashed as soon as my head hit the pillow and woke up twelve hours later, still high at one in the afternoon. I arose to the smell of John smoking weed and laughing uproariously in the living room. Jessica, who was smart enough to avoid the whole space cake situation, turned and said, "He's been like this all morning. I want to kill him. He bought some hash last night and he's been pounding it into a thin paste so he can send it back to America." For the rest of our time in Amsterdam, John was completely baked, but the sad thing was that I was, too, after consuming just one measly space cake.

The night before we departed for New York, John stayed out all night again. "You only live once!" he announced as he set out for the Red Light District. I was sure he was going to come back maimed. At six in the morning, Jessica and I were in the shower, getting ready to head to the airport. At seven, John strolled through the door, drunk and high out of his mind.

Once again, I led an inebriated John through the streets of a foreign country. In the cab on the way to the airport, I asked him if he had any drugs, since security would certainly pick up on this stumbling, stoned American carrying a flask through customs. "I wouldn't worry about that, Greg," John said. "I smoked everything I had. I'm as clean as a whistle." I begged to differ.

While we were in the air headed back to New York, John turned to me with a sheepish look on his face. He held a bag of weed in his hands. "I forgot about this bag I bought last night in the Red Light District. I shoved it in my cargo pants and I just found it. What should I do?" "How the fuck should I know? Flush it down the toilet or something," I told him. "What are you, insane? I've gotten this far; I'm gonna take my chances." As we departed the plane, I told Jessica to keep her distance. There was no way this pothead was going to land us in jail.

A week after we arrived in New York, I received a mysterious birthday card from Amsterdam. When I opened it up, right in the middle of the card was a quarter-size, shit-brown piece of hash John had pummeled in that living room back in Amsterdam. Apparently, he was able to go to the post office and have the card mailed in the fuzzy haze he was in, while all I could do was walk into walls. As I smoked the hash in the comfort of my home and looked at the pictures of our trip later that night, I realized maybe John wasn't so bad to vacation with after all…

CHAPTER 31.

SKEEZE MAGNET

The first time I visited Costa Rica, I realized that wherever I go, I will attract freaks. This became apparent during a bus ride for a zip-lining excursion my boyfriend, Paul, and I went on. After we piled into a bus at 8AM, I made the discovery that I would be sitting next to Ken, a 45 year-old science teacher with green teeth who kept reading double-entendres into everything I said. When the driver pulled a strange leaf off a tree for us to touch on the way to the site, I passed it to him and said, "This feels weird." "I hear that a lot," he said while leering at me. When he made us pass around a banana, he winked and said, "Mmmm. Thick."

A few hours later, the two of us wound up getting stuck on a platform high in the rain forest after the rest of the tour had zip lined to the next station. He seized on this opportunity to brush up against me. After running his tongue over the gaping hole between his two front teeth, he blew his garlic breath on me and said, "So, do you guys like to swing?"

"Only on zip lines," I said, and slid to my safety over the canopy of the rain forest.

CHAPTER 32.

FOLLOW YOUR BLISS

I never thought the Weather Girls would bring about an earth-shattering change in my life, but they did. The fact that this realization came as "It's Raining Men" played in a dimly lit gay bar in Rio makes the whole thing even more embarrassing, but you can't really plan for fate to step into your life. It just happens. At least that's what I tell myself to justify the fact that life-altering events happen in my life via The Weather Girls.

This epiphany took place during the Winter of 2003, when I went to Rio de Janeiro with my boyfriend, Paul, and our friend John, for vacation. An alcoholic through and through, John refused to go to sleep unless he was drunk, so each night, he dragged us to a bar so he could drink enough Imperial beer and shots of "SoCo chilled with a splash of lime juice" until he was soused enough to sleep. Then he'd head back to his room, open a bottle of red wine and drunk-dial friends in America from the bathroom as he smoked cigarettes on the toilet. Or call us up and demand we meet him on the roof deck with beer from our mini-fridge for a "night cap" after his stash ran out. When we refused, he'd scream through the phone,

"We're in Rio for Christ Sake's, not Jerusalem!" and make a few more calls until his cigarettes ran out. Without fail, every morning Paul would pull him through the lobby as I convinced the tour bus driver to wait "just one more minute" before heading out to Corcovado or the beaches of Ipanema.

Amazingly, John never complained about being hung over, as long as he got one cup of sugary tea and a pack of Parliaments. By noon, he'd order the requisite Imperial with lunch and that would be the end of it. But when midnight rolled around, there was no stopping him. He was like a Gremlin. He'd beg and plead until one of us went out for a drink, and I'd always cave in because I knew I'd come back with stories. Like the time he threw up underneath the bar and continued drinking as if nothing happened. "It was more like a glorified burp," he said as he ordered another beer. Or that time he threw up in a pint glass and placed the contents in a potted plant at the end of the bar. Or that time he threw up in his mouth and kept talking as if I didn't notice. Come to think of it, John did a lot of regurgitating. Thankfully, there was none during our trip to Rio. At least that I knew of.

We found a great bar not three blocks from our hotel the first night we went out. It was small and intimate, and held about twenty-five people. The owner, a theatrical man by the name of Antonio, used to direct soap operas, and had a flair for the dramatic. He named the bar The Blue Angel, after the movie starring Marlene Dietrich, and had posters of old films all over the bar. Blue lights illuminated the entire space. We quickly bonded with Antonio and the bartender, who loved to hear John's stories about working on Broadway and whatever I was able to get in about working in film and TV, which wasn't much after John got his first shot of SoCo…

Since Antonio worked in entertainment, the bar was always filled with the most interesting array of actors, actresses, and designers. His friends always stopped in for a drink, and over the course of the week, we befriended a hilarious costume designer named Rodrigo and a glamorous transsexual soap opera star named Gloria. I've yet to figure out why the words "transsexual" and "star" only seem to go together in Latin countries, although thanks to Caitlyn Jenner, that's finally starting to change.

Every night at one AM, Antonio would bust out the microphone; tell a few jokes and introduce a drag queen who entertained the crowd with impromptu performances. Although these drag queens worked hours on their hair and makeup, for some reason, the idea of shaving their forearms, back and armpits was lost on them. They all looked like gorillas in Marilyn Monroe wigs.

Later in the week, as the three of us were in the middle of asking Gloria questions about her operations, Antonio called me over after his opening monologue and told the crowd I would be performing. I was shocked, since I gave this man no clue I had any performing experience. I usually like to let people do all the talking when I meet them so I can write stories about them later on.

Ten seconds later, a spotlight hit me. I had no idea what to expect as he shoved the microphone in my hand. Any and all expectations were thrown out the window when "It's Raining Men" started playing. Convinced this was a joke, I decided I would have the last laugh. I switched over to performance mode and committed to the song with all my heart. As the first verse hit, I was in rare form –

sashaying up and down the bar, singing to patrons and climbing up the ladder that led to the loft where they stored the beer. By the time the second chorus kicked in, I ripped off my shirt and turned the performance into a full-on strip tease. I ended the song by jumping on the lap of Gloria in my underwear. I then exited dramatically…into the bathroom.

I was thrilled! I was excited! I was filled with all of the energy that comes from a thrilling! exciting! performance. As I re-entered the bar to gather my clothes from the floor, Antonio ran over and hugged me. "I knew you were a performer! I saw it in your eyes the minute I met you!" he said. So this wasn't some cruel joke. "That was incredible! I hope to some day be as good as you!" the 18-year old bartender told me. Were these people drunk? Yes. But that didn't change the fact that they saw me for the star I was! Now if only I could get my pants back on.

At this point in my life, I had given up acting years ago. Since then, I had concentrated on writing and directing films while working at *Saturday Night Live*. Years had passed since I went on stage to perform my first one man show, "Man-A-Thon." After that, I made a conscious decision *not* to pursue acting because although I loved it, I was a relatively well-adjusted person who didn't have the ***DRIVE*** and ***NEED*** for the world to love me. These are crucial elements I believe all actors need as years pass by and your only break is getting cast on an episode of *CSI* as Corpse #3.

But deep inside, ***I LOVED PERFORMING***! All this time, I was denying my true calling, and tonight, Martha Wash and Izora Rhodes made me realize what I was missing! I was filled with so much energy, *and I wanted more of it!* But as most people know, only like one percent of actors are able to support themselves through acting. Or at least that's what I had told myself…

As I went to bed that night, I got to thinking. All my life, I wanted to go to Rio. For some reason, I was drawn to that city. Other people loved Paris, or London, but I always wanted to go to Rio. I was obsessed with Bossa Nova and had pictures of the city in my apartment. Did the universe draw me to this city to remind me of what my true calling was? Yes, I decided it had.

I waited before making any changes, since I didn't want to be seen as a flake – you know, that friend of yours who decides they want to be a florist, then an interior designer and then wind up becoming a real estate broker at 45? I spoke with actor friends to see how they were able to make ends meet and how they felt about auditioning for twelve years without catching a break. Everyone knew why I was asking, and burst at the seams when I told them what I was thinking.

Instead of telling me I was crazy to leave a job that paid well and gave me ample time to work on creative projects, they were thrilled. At first I saw everyone's excitement as support, but years later, realized they were probably hoping they'd have someone else to commiserate with about how much acting can **SUCK ASS**.

When I spoke to non-creatives about this decision, I was met with a little more resistance. Paul thought I was completely insane to quit my job and jump into acting like **that**! We had just purchased a condo and my timing was not exactly ideal. I told him I would finish my season at *SNL* and segue into acting full time over the course of the year. In that time, I would work on getting an agent who would help me land paying gigs. Once again, my naïve Aries nature was leading the way!

My first step was getting new headshots. After 400 shots, *there it was*! That *one* picture where I didn't have complete and total gay face! A week later, I held the black and white 8X10's in my hand, ready to be mailed to agents and casting directors across the metro area. The only problem was that I was still working in production, and would have no time to audition if and when I *did* land an agent.

I decided I would be my own agent, and submit myself through Backstage, Craigslist, and Actors Access, that way I could work auditions around my schedule. Looking back, I highly recommend this approach if you want to meet every single freak in New York City. But at the time, my plan was to shoot as many films as I could, so I could get enough clips to build an acting reel. By the end of that first month, I was being called in all the time! For some reason, I kept getting cast as the tough guy from Brooklyn. I wanted to tell them, "Gurl, please" but I didn't mind. Every role was a chance to get another clip for my reel!

I joined AFTRA, which set me back $1300, but allowed me to do extra work, along with stand-in work on awards shows. One month later, there I was! At Radio City, improvising acceptance speeches at Tony Awards rehearsals to the tune of $92.00. Come November, I was standing in for the host of "The Macy's Thanksgiving Parade" and taking home another check...for $92.00.

I was able to land some more work, so I felt like I was ahead of the game. $768 ahead of the game. How did people make a living doing this, I wondered? The answer was: They didn't. Most actors I knew were waiters, masseuses, dog walkers, prostitutes and part-time prostitutes. That's how they earned their money. Not from playing a hot dog vendor on *Law & Order*.

As my season at *SNL* came to a close, I finally got to complete my acting reel...after hounding the God-damned directors to send me the shitty fucking films I acted in for five damned days eating dogcrap pizza the whole fucking time. I was already getting bitter, and I was only doing this on the side.

That's when a realization hit me: Although I loved acting, I didn't love the lifestyle that came with it. Besides having to compete for roles, I also had to deal with imbeciles who didn't know I worked in film and TV. Most days, I spent my time coaching AD's how to wrangle extras in office scenes and convincing neighbors not to call the police. Acting as a career was not for me. But doing it for pleasure was. So I decided I'd go back to writing and directing projects I could act in. That way, I would be assured to get cast in a role I was right for and only have to deal with my own incompetence. Then the internet happened, and I found the perfect outlet to perform and utilize my production skills on YouTube.

The fact that my first online successes featured this horse-faced man in drag made me realize it would have been a lot easier if I had skipped all that acting garbage, thrown on a wig and lip synced to Beyonce, which was obviously what the city of Rio was trying to tell me when I pranced around half-naked to The Weather Girls all those years ago...

ABOUT THE AUTHOR

Photograph by © Greg Endries

Greg Scarnici is a comedic artist and musician whose music video and commercial parodies have been viewed over 10 million times on YouTube and a host of other sites. His work has also been featured on MTV, VH1, Fox News and CNN. TV credits include appearances on *30 Rock, Online Nation, Nick Cannon: Short Circuitz*, and *Saturday Night Live*, where he currently works as an Associate Producer. Other TV writing credits include The Macy's 4th of July Fireworks Spectaculars on NBC and the 2014 NBA All-Star Pre-Game Concert. Film credits include writing and directing the award-winning indie, "Glam-Trash," and the short films, "Dead End," and "Children Of The Dune." Check out www.gregscarnici.com to see some of his work and to hear some of the music he has released as himself, his drag alter ego, Levonia Jenkins, and his band, Undercover.